Cambridge Elements ≡

Elements in Histories of Emotions and the Senses
edited by
Jan Plamper
Goldsmiths, University of London

SCHOLASTIC AFFECT

Gender, Maternity and the History of Emotions

Clare Monagle
Macquarie University, Sydney

T0364229

CAMBRIDGE
UNIVERSITY PRESS

CAMBRIDGE
UNIVERSITY PRESS

University Printing House, Cambridge CB2 8BS, United Kingdom

One Liberty Plaza, 20th Floor, New York, NY 10006, USA

477 Williamstown Road, Port Melbourne, VIC 3207, Australia

314–321, 3rd Floor, Plot 3, Splendor Forum, Jasola District Centre, New Delhi – 110025, India

79 Anson Road, #06–04/06, Singapore 079906

Cambridge University Press is part of the University of Cambridge.

It furthers the University's mission by disseminating knowledge in the pursuit of education, learning, and research at the highest international levels of excellence.

www.cambridge.org
Information on this title: www.cambridge.org/9781108814263
DOI: 10.1017/9781108886406

First published 2020

A catalogue record for this publication is available from the British Library.

ISBN 978-1-108-81426-3 Paperback
ISSN 2632-1068 (online)
ISSN 2632-105X (print)

Scholastic Affect

Gender, Maternity and the History of Emotions

Elements in Histories of Emotions and the Senses

DOI: 10.1017/9781108886406
First published online: August 2020

Clare Monagle
Macquarie University, Sydney
Author for correspondence: Clare Monagle, clare.monagle@mq.edu.au

Abstract : Scholastic theologians made the Virgin Mary increasingly perfect over the Middle Ages in Europe. Mary became stainless, offering an impossible but ideologically useful vision of womanhood. This Element offers an implicit theory of the utility and feelings of women in a Christian salvationary economy. The Virgin was put to use as a shaming technology, one that silenced and effaced women's affective lives. The shame still stands to this day, although in secularized mutated forms. This Element deploys the intellectual history of medieval thought to map the moves made in codifying Mary's perfection. It then uses contemporary gender and affect theory to consider the implications of Mary's perfection within modernity, mapping the emotional regimes of the medieval past upon the present.

Keywords: Virgin Mary, scholastic theology, history of emotions, gender, feminism, affect theory

ISBNs: 9781108814263 (PB), 9781108886406 (OC)
ISSNs: 2632-1068 (online), 2632-105X (print)

Contents

The Emotional Bind

It is so hard to write about emotions. Writing their history forces us into a bind. We want to find out how people in the past actually felt. We are also always aware of the vast gulf between ourselves and our subjects. Historical actors come to us through words and images that are themselves mediations of feeling. We reconstruct their worlds, we trouble over their accounts of their times and their selves, and we make our best attempts to do justice to their reality. We make them as alive as we can, but these attempts reveal as much distance as they do proximity. We cannot resurrect feelings; we can only reconstitute their manifestations in the realm we call 'culture'.

This is the historicism in which I was trained. As a medievalist, I was taught that the Middle Ages were neither barbarically other to modernity nor the laboratory within which modernity was founded. The period was merely itself, in spite of bearing a name that declared it to be a temporal rupture between the classical and the modern. Medieval Europe was diverse and complex and was governed by complicated logics, as is any historical period, and my job as its investigator was to learn the protocols necessary to make sense of this past world. I was trained to let the Middle Ages be its own place and time, as much as is possible, and to try to work out how it worked.

My particular focus has been scholastic theology. Scholastic theology was the queen of the disciplines in the universities and the *studia generalia* in Northern Europe. The project of scholasticism began in the twelfth century and was devoted to the codification and organisation of Christian doctrine. The object of these men, and they were all men, was to deploy scripture and patristic sources to build a cogent and coherent set of doctrines suitable to the age. They used dialectical reason to do so, attempting to integrate a diverse tradition of texts and opinions. In so doing, inevitably, they produced theological novelty. For example, to explain the regularly occurring miracle of the Eucharistic transformation of bread and wine into the body and blood of Christ, they had to assess the myriad theories that had transpired over a thousand years of Christian thinking. Eventually they came up with a neologism to make sense of the process, a type of scientific label, that of transubstantiation. This was the type of transformation afforded by scholastic theology, the formalisation and intellectualisation of doctrine. They produced orthodoxy, that is, right doctrine.

So I tried to make sense of how these theologians made sense of their world. I tried to relate their very complex inquiries to the world of their making. Why were they so driven to master their tradition? What were the drivers of the practices of thinking, and the institutions that housed them? And I tried to see how their hegemonic discourse remade that same world. What was the impact of this theology on practices of governance in the Middle Ages? How did scholastic theology work as a new technology of power? How was it used? What did it police? In making orthodoxy, what then became heresy? My point was not to excavate what they wrote, to recapitulate their positions on the Trinity or on the incarnation. Instead, I was interested in the work that their thought did in the making of norms, in the production of what would come to seem like the natural order of things in Western Europe, the idea of Christendom (Monagle 2017).

As I was doing this work, I encountered the history of emotions. I was not led to emotions through this work. Earlier in my career, it seemed to me that the deep distance between myself and my period of study precluded anything but a forensic approach to the texts to which I had access. For the most part, sources that survive from medieval theology are highly formal, since this was a practice that excluded all except for clerical elites. I searched for what my supervisor Gabrielle Spiegel called the 'social logic of the text', confident that discussions of emotions or affect were safely out of my remit (Spiegel 1990). I came to emotions, initially, for pragmatic reasons. Between 2011 and 2018, the Australian Research Council funded a Centre of Excellence in the History of Emotions (CHE), with a particular focus on European history between the years 1100 and 1800. CHE was based at the University of Western Australia but was led by researchers from across the nation. The well-funded CHE got to work; during its funded years, it organised a score of events that brought a great many researchers together to think about emotions.

And so many of us in Australia, even someone like myself who was quite tangentially linked to CHE, turned to emotions for reasons of both funding and access to the vibrant scholarly community offered by the CHE. At the beginning of this process, I was not prepared to take an emotional swerve. My entire intellectual formation, really, had taken place within the linguistic turn. I was gripped by the attempt to understand words in context, but also certain that those words could never be a direct representation of the things they described. I now see that this conviction was itself a historical one; I had been taught to experience and to perceive emotions as ineffable, as fleeting and embodied rather than real and cognitive. But at the time, my conviction as to the essential irreducibility of emotions was one that I thought I shared with my historical subjects, scholastic theologians. Language, they argued, was what we used to shape our apprehension of the world, but it was not the world itself. God had granted humans language, but it could not represent him entirely, only timorously. And since he, God, was ultimately the only true thing, language was always going to fail. It was grace rather than words that enabled the distance between God and man to be brokered. My scepticism about language was not based in theology as it was in the scholastics but emerged instead out of post-structuralist political thought, as well as through feminist psychoanalytic theory. This type of thinking suggested to me that the idea of a cogent self who can see and represent the world with clarity and accuracy was an intellectual and psychic fantasy. Instead of thinking of words as things that I could use, I thought of words as agents that worked on me. There was no me that was inviolably separate from discourse; I was not a self who told the truth. Rather, naturalised ideologies worked within me to produce an idea of self that was invariably fragile, even when I felt robust or clear. So if I knew that I could not tell the truth, that my words were not a representation of reality, how could I imagine that historical texts could do so? If I could not find integrity in my own emotions and represent them accurately, how could historical texts possibly do so? So, I resisted the history of emotions because it seemed to me that all the field could possibly do was tell the story of how stories have been told about emotions. As I understood it, emotions themselves could not possibly be a category of analysis, only their representation. I know better now, or at least I know differently. My initial resistance to emotions depended upon a set of oppositions that I was insistent on maintaining, between body and mind, conscious and unconscious, self and other, thinking and feeling, past and present.

So what changed? Why am I now writing this Element in a series titled 'Histories of Emotions and the Senses'? What is the nature of my conversion? There are two answers to this question: one is personal and one is scholarly. In this Element, in the text that follows, I hope to show that those categories are not as separate as we usually make them, and that understanding the ways that they bleed into each other is significant work. Firstly, I became a mother in 2004 and giving birth to my daughter remains the most shocking thing that has ever happened to me. Honora's birth was truly terrible and left me with lasting physical and psychic trauma, which will be with me for the rest of my life. The birth also, however, resulted in her coming into the world, the most quotidian and marvellous of miracles. In the days after her birth, I celebrated her being with complete joy while mourning the wreckage of myself. Nothing in my psychological arsenal had prepared me to confront ambivalence on that scale. I am still reeling, in 2020, although thankfully without the terror that accompanied those early days. At that time, I thought a great deal about how we understand motherhood in the West, and what resources might help me make sense of what had just happened. And, since I had been brought up in a Catholic family, my mind kept turning to the Virgin Mary. I remembered countless beatific images of Mary with the infant Christ, in which Mary tenderly gazes upon her stunning boy. That I should do so is unsurprising, as the feminist philosopher Adriana Cavarero has noted 'the scenario of birth' has been 'culturally requisitioned and hyperrepresented by the Christian iconology of nativity' (Cavarero 2014, 23). I also remembered, as I thought about Mary, that scholastic theologians had insisted that Mary did not experience pain in childbirth. Since pain in childbirth was a punishment issued to women as a result of the Fall, and as she had been spared the pain of original sin, Mary did not suffer as the rest of us must. In my febrile post-partum musings, I became furious as I realised properly, with visceral anger, that the most important and visible mother in the history of Western culture was celebrated precisely because she had not been broken by birth. I realised that it was not merely that birthing had been ignored in the Western tradition but also that a great deal of work had gone into its denial. Mary was the most visible part of a larger refusal on the part of Western thought to engage with birthing particularly, and maternity generally. As the feminist philosopher Christine Battersby has noted, 'there were very few philosophers prior to the feminist philosophers who took birth into account in the analysis that they offered of freedom, self-identity, virtue or the good life' (Battersby 1998, 17). I was having what I am clumsily calling a 'feeling-knowledge', encountering the intellectual traditions of Western thought anew, and registering their exclusions in my gut and in my heart.

Back in 2004, I had no idea what to do with this new feeling-knowledge I had acquired in new motherhood. For the most part, as a young would-be scholar, I put the anger away and tried to get on with work and reclaim my old self. It was too confusing to do otherwise. In the introduction to her classic *Of Woman Born*, Adrienne Rich wrote about why it took her such a long time to write about maternity. She had to reckon with the profoundly ambivalent work of motherhood, the hybrid feelings of love and fear and fatigue that seem to threaten psychic integrity and undo the self. To speak of and in motherhood, Rich said, she needed to 'return to a ground which seemed to me the most painful, incomprehensible and ambiguous I had ever travelled, a ground hedged with taboos, mined with false-namings' (Rich 1976, 15). To confront the experience of birth, and the transformative knowledge-feeling that emerges, took Rich a great many years. It takes time to recognise and undo taboos. Taboos work so powerfully because they feel natural, and to cross them arouses unbearable shame. 'The motherhood of scholars is forbidden', Jill Lepore has written, and she is not just referring to structural issues pertaining to childcare and lactation rooms (Lepore 2019). She is speaking of motherhood as a scholarly taboo, in terms of both subject matter and identity. Scholars look at something from elsewhere and use their brains to turn data into a coherent and bounded story. They deploy their critical faculties to find patterns out of chaos, and to find meaning in mess. But birth is mess; it is a space of profound interdependence, and it must be abject to be. This is why, perhaps, the scholarly work that does deal with birth in the humanities and social sciences tends to the ethical, to demarcating what reproductive rights should be afforded to women, and to understanding the sexual politics of those who seek to deny them. But to write about birth itself, as that which refuses all the distance we claim as scholars, that is another project entirely, and one for which it is almost impossible to find the words.

That was the personal part of my road to Damascus account of my turn to emotions, my experience of being undone by birth and inaugurated into this new feeling-knowledge. In a practical scholarly sense, however, my conversion occurred much later through my participation in the aforementioned CHE. It was in the myriad conversations that took place under its auspices that I was forced to encounter the rigidity of the historicism to which I clung. Because 'the motherhood of scholars is forbidden', I had not allowed the transformation of birth to penetrate my work; instead, I had cordoned it away and held even more tightly to the fantasy of intellectual distance. But at CHE events, I encountered scholars who insisted on the need to talk about emotions in the past, and the present, even if in doing so we risk projecting ourselves onto our subjects and universalising emotions very particular to time and place. We need to do this because we know that people feel, and that they have done so across time and culture. This sounds so reductive and does a great disservice to the complexity of the field, but to me it was a revelation. The history of emotions need not work out what people actually felt, but it takes the reality of feeling as a foundation for understanding the past. And this means, and here is the biggest challenge, if we let feelings be real, as scholars we have to own up to our own. These avowals do not come easy for historians. In a parallel example, Emily Robinson has written about the deployment of memory studies by historians that 'much as they study the construction, dynamics and persistence of "collective memory", historians seem to be embarrassed to turn their attention to their own relationship with the past' (Robinson, 2010, 505). The fantasy I had held on to, that I could be disembodied in scholarship and keep my body for home life, had sustained me for a long time. But the history of emotions helped me understand that this was not a natural divide and was one that was damaging to myself and to scholarship. Because the ideal of the dispassionate scholar is one, really, only permitted or available to the white rational male. Masculine ideals might change historically, as do ideas about what might constitute his whiteness or his rationality, but what has not changed in the intellectual history of the West is the idea of the man of reason as constitutive of proper thinking itself. As Genevieve Lloyd has it, 'rationality has been conceived as transcendence of the feminine; and the "feminine" itself has been partly constituted by its occurrence within this structure' (Lloyd 1984, 104). For those us who are not men of reason, we occupy scholarly space on borrowed time, and when we do so we prop it up, we keep the taboo active that precludes the fleshed and the wounded from scholarship.

And so I feel like I am starting afresh with this Element, *Scholastic Affect: Gender, Maternity and the History of Emotions*. In this volume, I want to look at the history of medieval theology, particularly that which pertains to the Virgin Mary, to consider the boundaries it marks, its constitution of the feminine, and to see how its preoccupations are still with us today. This is not the story of affective piety in the Middle Ages, a field which has its own rich scholarship (Crocker 2017). *Scholastic Affect* is interested instead in the often very unemotional discourse of the male theologians who constructed the rational Christian male as the default subject in the West. Feminist work in the history of philosophy has excavated the man of reason as he obtains in philosophy, but true to the periodization of their discipline, they have tended to ignore the Middle Ages as part of that account. The occlusion of the medieval means the missing of the Virgin Mary. This is some loss, because scholastic theology made Mary perfect over the course of the Middle Ages. They theorised her virginity, explained how she avoided the pains of childbirth, and finally how she herself was spiritually without stain. In so doing, of course, they correlated women's abject bodies as being particularly implicated in sin, making them especially unfit to access reason. The natality at the heart of the Christian story was sanitised by scholasticism, relegating the reality of women's sexed bodies to the theological offstage. Scholastic theology deplored mess. The scholastic project aimed to tighten doctrine through logic, to make it unassailable. Women were put to that work, in that they were excluded from it, made invisible.

I still live in the world that they made, and I still feel the impact of scholasticism as shaming technology, an idea that I will discuss further in the Element. In *Scholastic Affect*, I am not only going to describe medieval theologies of the Virgin Mary, I am also going to meditate upon their meanings in my own life, and in the cultural world I inhabit. This is the other debt to which I owe the CHE; it was under its auspices that I first began to engage with affect theory. Affect theory excited me not because of its attempts to examine the precognitive attachments we bring to the world, but because it models a new way of writing the self into the historicisation of emotions. As Sara Ahmed has described, we are oriented in our worlds, and we orient to things (Ahmed 2006). Affect theory, in the vein of Ahmed, encourages us to encounter our orientations, and to trace what they make possible in our work as scholars. For Ahmed, affect is sticky; it binds emotions together and produces feelings of coherence, the 'I' that enables us to be. In particular, Ahmed suggests that rather than pursuing emotions in an isolated psychological frame, they must be reckoned with in context. She says that 'we need to consider how they work, in concrete and particular ways, to mediate the relationship between the psychic and the social, and between the individual and the collective' (Ahmed 2004, 119). She argues that emotions do their work relationally and ideologically, always imbricated in regimes of power and bodies both subjected and resistant. She aims to 'show how emotions work by sticking figures together (adherence), a sticking that creates the very effect of a collective (coherence)' (Ahmed 2004, 119). I oriented to the study of scholastic theology as a young woman, because I urgently needed to understand the Catholic world in which I grew up, and to make sense of the gendered theology through which my parents had refracted the world to me. I left the Church as soon as I could, at around eighteen; yet, my deepest and most tender sense of being in the world was still, shamefully, infused with the sacramental regime of my childhood. It still sticks; I am still stuck. I cannot read scholastic theology without fury about its sexual policing; yet, I feel deeply at home with its words. These are my people. So, *Scholastic Affect* is about my emotions too, my love and my resistance. In this account, the Virgin Mary retains the status of mediator that she holds in Catholic theology. But rather than mediating between God and man, this Mary mediates between present and past, and between the scholar and her historical subjects.

This toggling between past and present, this invocation to understand how things stick and how being stuck feels, means that this Element will not unfold with characteristic scholarly precision. While I will offer an account of how Marian scholastic theology understands and manages Mary, and how this changes over the course of the Middle Ages, I will also animate this history with excursions into the now. These may be jarring, deliberately so. I will be talking about Miley Cyrus when I talk about virginity, and Jordan Peterson when I talk about purity, for example. My now is globalised and Western, postcolonial and Antipodean. The scholastic theology that I explicate remains meaningful in this now because its version of womanhood still obtains in myriad ways across these cultures in which I live. This is not to say the theologians caused the present day; it is to say that we encounter them in the now, and that the accord and discord between them and us might help us dwell as historical beings in the knottiness of our genealogies.

Introduction The Maternal Scholar

Peter Lombard's *Sentences*, written around 1156, was the core textbook used in theological training in Europe from the twelfth until the sixteenth centuries. In that work, Lombard surveyed and synthesised Christian teachings, producing a schema of doctrine. The *Sentences* offered neither the temporal nor the spiritual narrative of the two books of the Bible. Rather, the textbook extrapolated the meanings offered by the Bible into useable pieces of knowledge. For example, Lombard taught that marriage should indeed be reckoned a sacrament, as multiple biblical examples convey God's support for sanctioned conjugal unions. Would Christ have transformed the water into wine at the wedding of Cana were he not in favour of the celebration? In Lombard's text, the stories of the Bible were edified into teachings to be apprehended. And that was, overall, the project of scholastic theology throughout the Middle Ages. The task of theological training was to enable the scholar to move from sacred scripture, and the myriad meditations of the patristic fathers upon scripture, towards a structure of knowing, an architecture of doctrine (Colish 1994).

I have been working on Lombard's *Sentences* for fourteen years, a time frame easily remembered as it coincided with the infancy of my daughter. I began studying the text, the subject of my doctoral dissertation, as my baby came into the world of signs and touch, of meaning and separation. Watching her vulnerability turned me inside out, *vulnus* is, after all, the Latin word for 'wound'. In 'Stabat Mater', Julia Kristeva described the shock of the infant's emergence into being, and the new world they inaugurate for the mother. She wrote that 'one does not bear children in pain, it's pain that one bears; the child is pain's representative and once delivered, moves in for good.' The baby's first breath anticipates their last, and this knowledge, according to Kristeva, exposes the mother to the acute sublimity of abjection. She admits that deferral of this new pain suffices to some degree, 'obviously you can close your eyes, stop up your ears, teach courses, run errands, clean house, think about things, about ideas' (Kristeva 1985, 138). But deferral cannot heal and restore; it can only displace and move the pain around.

For me at least, that was about the sum of it. The act of bearing and nourishing this little one had me in what felt like a temporal vice; the past was gone forever and the future frighteningly unknown. Now, in retrospect, I think I was in what we could call a 'bloom space', to borrow a term from Kathleen Stewart (Stewart, 2010). In a bloom space, we are in past and future, hinging between selves. Bloom spaces feel out of time; however, when we are in them, we are deeply in time, caught between who we imagined ourselves to be in the past and knowing that the present and the future will require a yet unimagined form of flourishing or abatement. A bloom space is 'a promissory note. An allure and a threat that shows up in ordinary sensibilities of not knowing what compels' (Stewart 2010, 340). In mothering an infant, a life of myriad abjections and inevitable recursion into my own infancy, a new reality was inaugurated in which affect was cause and symptom and solution. This was the shock of the new, but it was a new that seemed to be eternal and primordial. There is no new thing under the sun, but nothing was the same.

I worked on the aforementioned Lombard as part of the obfuscating strategy described by Kristeva earlier. Scholastic theology enabled me to close my eyes and stop up my ears. Scholastic theologians were *magistri*, masters, who promised a totalising competency. The truth was out there, they thought, held in trust on the sacred page and in the book of nature. God-given human ingenuity, infused with faith, could unlock this truth and transform it into knowledge. In his *Sic et Non*, Abelard claimed that virtuous doubt could unlock the *clavis sapientiae*, the keys of wisdom (Smalley 1981). Between 1150 and 1520, scholastic inquiry was the master discourse of Western Europe. Even philosophy was understood to be subordinate to theology. In universities across the continent, scholars followed Abelard's injunction and interrogated their tradition so that they could capture the keys to wisdom, lawfully entering into sacred knowledge. The subject of my research was one of those moments of questioning on the part of the schoolmen. In his *Sentences*, Lombard had asked 'Whether Christ, according to his being a man, is a person or anything'? That is, what is the status of Christ's humanity? Can Christ's humanity be reified as a thing? And if it can, does that undermine his divinity? But if Christ's humanity is not a thing, a nothing, then what of the incarnation? Lombard was not able to settle upon the *quidditas* of Christ's humanity, but his doubting question was debated for subsequent centuries and led to refinement of theological vocabulary, as well as forging discussions as to what type of thing humanity might be (Monagle 2013). It was in these debates, in these universalising and yet abstruse medieval conversations, that I tried to distance myself from the bloom space generated by intimate proximity to infancy. It was a profound relief, in the squealing seeping contracted world of her survival, to enter the world where humanity could be imagined to be a concept that could be defined and bounded.

That the schoolmen had little to say about maternal experience will surprise no one at all. And I certainly was not looking to medieval theological treatises to bridge the gap between work and home. But it has always stayed with me that Kristeva wrote those eloquent words about motherhood and pain within a larger essay concerned with how medieval thinkers produced Mary, mother of God, in theologically appropriate terms. 'Stabat Mater' takes its title from a thirteenth-century hymn devoted to the contemplation of Mary as she stood alongside her son, 'her sweet child', as he suffered on the cross. Kristeva follows medieval thinkers as they produce a cordon sanitaire around Mary's messy humanity, producing her inviolable perfection. As scholastic theology flourishes in the high Middle Ages, so too does popular Marian devotion, necessitating elite management. In 1100, it was considered an error to claim that Mary herself was free from sin, born from Immaculate Conception. Two hundred years later, Duns Scotus who was the pre-eminent scholar of his day and who served as an advisor to the French king, developed stringent theological arguments as to the necessity of her conception without stain. Medieval thinkers spent a great deal of time thinking about maternity, in fact, and they tore themselves into a great many logical knots trying to work out how it could be sanctified. Just as they had to work out the status of Christ's humanity, they had to grapple with the meaning of his human maternity. Could Mary have suffered in childbirth? Did Jesus need to be born a boy? Was Jesus ever naughty? Did the holy family chuckle? To perform his radical saving work, Christ needed to be human; he needed to suffer as we have suffered. However, to perform his radical saving work, Christ needed to be God; he needed to be our perfect creator.

When I describe this vein of scholastic questioning to students or colleagues, they are intrigued and bemused. How silly these medieval thinkers seem to us in their obsession with taxonomizing, in their deadly precise language, the diurnal and nocturnal humanity of Christ. In those moments, I like to respond by quoting from a surprising source, Will Ferrell's character Ricky Bobby, from the 2006 comedy *Talladega Nights*. Ricky Bobby is a race car driver, who has overcome hardship and pain to conquer Daytona and receive riches and fame beyond expectation. He lives in a palatial mansion, his wife is suitably bomb-shell beautiful, and she has provided him with the children who complete his tableau of success. As all-conquering paterfamilias, Ricky Bobby proudly leads the family in grace before meals, exhorting them to pray to Jesus. It is to the infant Christ that Ricky Bobby directs his prayer, extolling.

> Dear tiny Jesus in your golden fleece diapers and with your tiny balled up fists. Dear eight pound, six ounce, newborn infant Jesus that don't even know a word yet, just a little infant, but still omnipotent. (Talladega Nights 2006)

The joke lands in both the absurdity of an all-powerful infant and our recognition of the putatively ignorant Ricky Bobby's theological acuity. The point of the incarnation is precisely this paradox – that omnipotence and humanity reside in the same hypostatic person. Ricky Bobby gets it. Of course scholastics were engaged in the minutiae of Christ's humanity, because the incarnation is the founding fact of Christianity: to know the human is to know God.

Childbirth gives us the baby, and it is this that is celebrated on Christmas Day, the safe arrival of the infant Jesus, ready to be worshipped. Childbirth also produces the mother. Mary too, of course, is celebrated on Christmas Day, in her radiant post-partum haze. But where we are happy and delighted to contemplate the squealing squawking carnal infant, we celebrate Mary's maternity in its non-carnality. Somehow, magically, she is pure and beatific, untroubled by what has transpired. She has not given birth to pain; she has painlessly given birth to salvation. Obviously, her experience is not typical. The new mother oozes, her body is porous, and it in turn cleaves to the infant and then separates from her. Few things can rigorously be said to be universal. That babies are born from bodies with wombs is one of those few things. And that this process is abject, dangerous, fraught, and very messy is another of those rare universals. And that it takes an enormous amount of utterly necessary life-preserving work to keep those babies alive for the first year of their life is also a transhistorical fact. Mary is kept outside of this danger, this risk, and this mess. This is some erasure. In the words of Marina Warner. 'Mary establishes the child as the destiny of woman, but does not experience the sexual intercourse necessary for all other women to experience this destiny.' (Warner 1976, 336). Likewise, she does not birth as other women.

As is well known, a core insight of feminism has been to reveal the systematic erasure of this work of maternity across Western culture, which moves far beyond the image of the Virgin's body. In 1976, Mary Kelly exhibited *Post-Partum Document*, her large-scale artwork that documented her son's infancy, which insisted that the occluded work of mothering had a rightful place as a subject of art, and that the effort of maternity had been hidden from public accounts of labour, value and worth. The artist wrote an introduction to the exhibition, which was exhibited alongside the artworks, in which she declared in caps:

> IN THE POST-PARTUM DOCUMENT, I AM TRYING TO SHOW THE RECIPROCITY OF THE PROCESS OF SOCIALIZATION IN THE FIRST FEW YEARS OF LIFE. IT IS NOT ONLY THE INFANT WHOSE FUTURE PERSONALITY FORMED AT THIS CRUCIAL MOMENT, BUT ALSO THE MOTHER WHOSE 'FEMININE PSYCHOLOGY' IS DEALED BY THE SEXUAL DIVISION OF LABOR IN CHILDCARE. (Kelly 1983, 1)

Kelly systematically documented the data of her son's first years, analysing his soiled nappies, documenting his feeds and recording the mimetic sonic interchanges between child and parents as he moved into language. She also mapped her transformation as a mother, writing clinical-like notes on the forms of anxiety, guilt and connection that now suffused her 'feminine psychology'. *Post-Partum Document* takes the normative forms of the treatise and the artwork and clinical observation, usually used to display mastery and distance, and insistently makes birthed and birthing bodies an object of analysis.

Post-Partum Document is denaturalising, while being about the 'natural', because it reminds us that maternity and infancy are not in fact mere abjection that should be confined to the realm of the private. There is a world of being and a world of meaning generated by Kelly's document that argues for the pre-eminent place of scatological and sensual natality as a philosophical topic. And this, in turn, forces the query, where has it been all this time? This is a question that has been asked of philosophy. Scholars such as the aforementioned Genevieve Lloyd, and Moira Gatens, have shown how philosophy itself is founded on an idea of reason that depends on the derogation of the feminine for its definition (Lloyd 1984; Gatens 1996). And when I think about that hideous wonderful time of caring for a newborn, I feel a great deal of relief at the refuge of reason scholarship seemed to offer, a consoling pleasure in its repudiation of the maternal. It was very comforting to think through categories and to build conceptual fortifications. In fact, Peter Lombard's *Sentences* offered an excellent case study in how to use reason to control the uncontrollable. In that book, Lombard imposed taxonomic order on the Christian tradition. He organised human knowledge, as he understood it, into four books. These books concerned, in this order, the trinity, the creation, the incarnation and the sacraments. He began with the concept of the trinity, the idea of the triune God that was developed in the centuries after Christ. He did not start with creation or natality, both of which were available to him and perhaps more self-evident as moments of beginning. Instead, Lombard insisted on proceeding to questions of the earth and of birth through the distancing technique of the Trinity. In so doing, he revolutionised theological training in particular, and Christian doctrine generally, in the West (Rosemann 2004).

This framing made the messy and accreted Christian story, that of lurid hagiographies, ghoulish relics and miracle stories, subordinate to the *ordo rationis*, the order of reason to which theology claimed privileged access (Monagle 2015). There was little room for Mary in this account. Peter Lombard worked at Notre Dame in Paris; he well understood the necessity of Our Lady in the world of Christian meaning. But she had little place in, or access to, the *ordo rationis* that undergirded his schema. Her example was meaningful – Lombard was interested particularly in her marriage to Joseph as a sacramental model. But her necessity to the Christian story was in no way a source of authority or meaning. The repressed, however, tends to return. And in the centuries that followed, the theologians who were trained with Lombard's textbook were forced to contend with the problem of Mary. Mary was popular. Stories were told and songs were sung about her miracles. Painters and sculptors depicted her with infant son, in so doing creating novel visual approaches to emotions and holiness. As Emma Maggie Solberg has recently explored, popular medieval representations of Mary, particularly in drama, revealed her to be ludic and dynamic: 'Mary was not always and is not always so vanilla'

(Solberg, 2018, 4). People prayed to her. They sought her help. She, alongside her wounded and broken son, became the subject of intense devotional and creative practices. She was volatile and potent. After Lombard, and in relation to the popular desire for Mary, theologians needed to bring her into the doctrinal system; she needed to be disciplined. Mary's pain could not be allowed to destroy the world; it needed to hold it up. As Jacqueline Rose has pointed out in relation to classical and medieval images of maternal suffering, 'the mother must be noble and her agony redemptive' (Rose 2018, 12). Her task is to be bulletproof and yet able to take the bullet of suffering at any moment. She suffers, but she resists its violations, its furies and its excess. This Element is, in part, the story of how scholastic theologians rationalised Mary's nobility and allegorised her agony. And, spoiler alert, they did this by making her more like God and less like a human. As I will show, they tied themselves in the most elaborate theological knots to do this. Their herculean efforts to make Mary reasonable reveal, I will argue, a stifling of her power to play, and to act.

Back to me. The scholastics mirrored (or perhaps helped produce) my own pathological anxiety about the maternal. Maternity is incontinent, literally and figuratively. It has to be – the baby is of the mother and the mother is of the baby. They contain each other, but neither is continent during birth and infancy. The conceit of scholarly practice, however, is that of continence. In his famous prayer, Augustine of Hippo had beseeched God, 'give me chastity and self-control' (Augustine 1998, 159). He was asking for help to hold himself in, to contain the supplements generated by ego and desire. As scholars, we try to contain the supplements around us, to turn them into something we can name and know. This is why I wanted to be a scholar: from the time I first went to university I was beguiled by the possibility of drawing order from chaos, of categorising the barrage of sensations, signs, appetites and stories that made me up as a human subject. It felt very noble and very hopeful. Maternity, however, refused my fantasy of order. It jolted me out of the *ordo rationis*, or at least that is what I thought and that was how it felt. There could be no more continence, and so I feared that there could be no more scholarship. My solution was denial, and so I kept on working on scholastic theology so that I could bear witness to its elaborate attempt to wrangle doctrine from mystery, facts from faith.

But if a system has no space for incontinence, no space for mess and maternity, then can it be anything other than life denying? And perhaps what we should try to understand as scholars is not how to contain the abject, but to try and notice all the places where the abject has been abjured. The discourses that denounce or deny the affective trembling of our beings are fascinating, not only for the knowledge they generate but also for the shame and the taboos at which they hint. *Scholastic Affect* is my attempt to explore the myriad occlusions of the real that occur in the production of the theology of Mary. The history of Western thought has been shown by feminist and postcolonial scholarship to have enshrined a man, a white man, of reason as the default subject. In that, medieval thought is no different. But because medieval theology is forced to deal with the problem of maternity due to the necessity of the Christian story, it is somewhat easier to locate its gendered anxieties than it would be in philosophy. The theologians make Mary perfect, and to do so they have to define what is normatively imperfect about women and about motherhood. For her to be a suitable mother to God, she needs to be cleaned up. She needs to be immaculate, which literally means without stain.

In affect studies, there has been a privileging of certain types of affects, those that seem to arrive unbidden and reveal something real that we have worked hard to sequester. For example, Ben Highmore says, 'Affect is what gives you away: the telltale heart; my clammy hands; the note of anger in your voice; the sparkle of glee in their eyes' (Highmore 2010, 118). This is recognisable; we know the moments when feeling gives something away, when the hint of a tear or the surge of a crowd seems to instantiate something that cannot be denied, that refuses to be buried. But affects circulate, and act, in regimes or ideologies or civilisations or communities. Affects do not act on us as if from outer space; they are as cultural as we are; they are us and we are relational. So what then of a world in which the affects of maternity – rich, terrifying, profound, life giving – are policed, forbidden and erased? And, in turn, what happens to the affects of maternity under those conditions? If I am right, that maternity is kind of everything, then it must take an inordinately phobic strength to keep it away, to privatise it and in fact to silence it. What is this strength, and what is this phobia? And, as scholars, we still live in the house that if these theologians did not make, they certainly helped to fortify. The first word of Lombard's *Sentences* is *cupientes*, which means 'desiring'. Desiring what? This is what I want to know: what is scholastic desire, and perhaps also what is scholarly desire? And where are the babies?

In a review of Jacqueline Rose's previously quoted *Mothers: An Essay on Love and Cruelty*, the novelist Tessa Hadley took aim at the book's sweeping claims. The argument of *Mothers* is that motherhood is used, in the West, as the place where we bury grievance, conflict and disgust. Mothers bear suffering acutely, in the manner pointed out by Kristeva, but they also must clean it up and make it manageable with the adroit application of Band-Aids and kissing it better. They are our culture's shock absorbers, living in the horrific sublime of the abject so that the rest of us do not have to. And for this labour, they are not accorded the status of sage, guru or CEO, even though they have corralled multitudes. Instead, their task is to re-present this mess – a mess which includes their own bodies – back to the world in a tidy state. Out damn spot – women on television clean the world as if it were a murder site. And their post-partum bodies are firm and bounded, ready and willing to resume sexual and scopic duties. In her review, Hadley asked Rose for more specifics: she wanted to know who makes motherhood what Rose describes. Hadley challenged Rose to provide an agent in her exploration of cultural logics; she asks 'who exactly is demanding that mothers be "love and goodness incarnate", "appease the wrongs of human history and the heart"?, all of us? The west? Men? Or only "right-wing politicians" (Hadley 2018).

Hadley's criticisms are tempting to dismiss. Rose writes as a psychoanalyst and cultural critic. Do we need to sweat the details, the tedium of working out how this has happened, and how it keeps on happening? If we keep looking and we keep seeing the same old things, what does the forensic search for agency achieve?

My answer is that we are not looking for an agent, that is, a responsible being or beings who know what they do. Hadley is seeking a prime mover, and in so doing she is reprising the Aristotelian idea of origins that was so integral to Aquinas's transformation of scholastic theology. In Aquinas's formulation, the prime mover was conflated with God. And since we had things in the world, since we had a world in fact, therefore we had proof of God. Nothing can be without a prime mover. I am; therefore, there is a God. To look for a prime mover is necessarily an act of reification; it makes something real by insisting that someone made it. This is what scholastic theology, after Aquinas, did. All the data of the world, every messy bit of it, was construed as evidence for and insight into the prime mover. And this is why I am resistant to Hadley's demands for the agent. The demand assumes that we can unpack our deep cultural confusion about maternity into something legible and bounded. We can assign responsibility, she implies, and therefore try to do things differently.

But feminist scholars have been explaining this for a long time. We have so many words and so much data about the how and why of our maternal refusals. Parts of the academy have worked so hard to produce the legibility demanded by Hadley. And policymakers and activists in the West have developed and implemented policies that support maternity, to some degree. But the meaning of the mother, the perfection that is expected of her and the demand that she privatise the mess have not changed. So I am not offering the following discussion of Mary as an origin story. I am not sure what it explains to our present predicaments, however construed. Rather, I am exposing a sediment in our cultural and intellectual histories, one that aims to console and encourage. We are not making it up. The incontinent abject mother is intolerable now, as she was in the Middle Ages. The work it took to make Mary perfect testifies to this.

And that is why I will keep myself in this story, because it is a form of testimony. Writing about maternity is as hard as writing about sex; the language is so clunky and turns the exquisite into the hackneyed. And yet, a great many of the foundational feminist thinkers who have rendered maternity visible have felt impelled to do so through personal accounting. At the start of *Of Women Born*, Adrienne Rich writes, 'It seemed impossible from the first to write a book of this kind without being autobiographical, without often saying "I"' (Rich 1976, 15). Kristeva, as we have seen, places her analysis of the making of the Immaculate Mary alongside a meditation of her own experiences of birthing and pain. Marina Warner, in *Alone of All Her Sex*, frames her exploration of the history of the Virgin through her own identification with Mary as a child, and the affective work Marian piety enabled her to do as a young woman (Warner 1976). Jacqueline Rose's work is suffused with her own experiences as an adoptive mother (Rose 2018). In so doing, these women offer themselves in two registers (Rose 2018). They juxtapose the schematic voice of the scholar with the poetic digressions of the mystic. They attempt to puncture linearity with exuberance, moving between the emic and the etic, the observed and the observer. They are not testifying to the sovereignty of the personal and offering an ontology of female flesh. They are testifying to the inexorable hold these distinctions have over the way we live as selves, and their seeming irreducibility. This type of feminist work does not offer the personal to trump the philosophical, but to reveal normative thought's blind spots, those things which are hiding in plain sight. I do not offer an account of experience to be authentic, but rather to be dialectical.

Writing in 1989 about a new wave of body-inflected feminisms, Moira Gatens, referring to the work of Elizabeth Grosz, argued, 'The "writing of the feminine body", far from being an exercise in feminist separatism, involves – and *necessarily* involves – addressing the other, the "thou" of our social relations' (Gatens 1996, 38–9, emphasis in original). Gatens suggested that thinking through the otherness produced by gender relations, in understanding how genders constitute each other through social and scopic regimes at once thrilling and oppressive, was a necessary beginning to 'creative and experimental attempts to transform ways of being male or female in the present or in the future' (Gatens 1996, 37). I started university in 1992, at Monash University where Elizabeth Grosz happened to be working at the time, and where there was a lot of Moira Gatens in the curriculum. I read Australian feminist philosophy at the same time as I read Lombard and Aquinas. It is a pretty weird combination, looked at from the bird's-eye view. But at the time it felt apposite. In scholastic theology, its epistemic power muted because I did not believe in the divine referent at its heart; I could see how elite men weaponised reason and guaranteed their own authority. In feminist philosophy, in its post-structural and psychoanalytic type, I found forgiveness for my love and desire for these regimes of reason and recognition. While not much can be said to be natural, Gatens et al. helped me to understand that what felt like a shameful lusting after the power and authority held by reason's gatekeepers made a type of sense, as did occasionally lusting after the men themselves to whom that task mostly fell. And they taught me that our task is not to pursue a utopian fantasy of the eradication of the gender order, or to the transcendence of difference. It is to attend to the gender order in which are made, to take stock of its libidinal power and understand our own investments in it, while furiously noting the asymmetrical punishments it doles out.

And the asymmetry of punishment is no accident; it has been there since the Fall, since Genesis. Scholastic theology, however, updated it to conform to Marian perfection. The Marian theology that gives us the perfect Virgin emerges, necessarily, from understanding the gendered consequences of the banishment from Eden. But scholastic readings of Genesis are themselves transformed by the saving work performed by Mary's body, and the need to make theological arguments for it. Aquinas explains that three curses fell on humanity as a result of the Fall, and that 'the first curse fell upon woman, that in conceiving she should lose her virginal integrity, that she should bear in difficulty and should bring forth in pain' (Every 1954, 35). This is an interesting gloss, in that Aquinas supplements the biblical text by naming loss of virginity as part of the punishment. He then tells us that 'the Blessed Virgin was immune from this pain and sorrow, for she conceived without losing her virginal integrity, bore in comfort and brought forth in joy the Saviour' (Every 1954, 35). The remaining two curses are equal opportunity. All humans are subject to the penalty of labour and death. But to woman alone falls the first of the curses; it is the curse of maternity. She must bear the children, but in conceiving them her virginity is destroyed, and virginity offers the only mode to integrity. And having forsaken integrity to conceive, she is then subject to the burden of pregnancy and the devastation of birth. The Bible and later interpreters are resolute about this. The whole thing is meant to be horrible and hard – God made it thus. Mary's immunity, what Duns Scotus would later call her privilege, did not provide an aspirational path. Rather, the figure of Mary symbolised the impossibility of women's transcendence. To be a woman was, necessarily, to be more sinful than a man. This could only be overcome when the sovereign exercised his right to declare an exception, and he had only done so once for Mary, and there was no hint that he was likely to do it again. This was an asymmetrical punishment, metered out by the gender order of medieval Europe.

Mary is no longer with us in the West as she once was – the Protestant Reformation took care of that to some degree. But the conditions of impossibility that she represents remain. In *Scholastic Affect: Gender, Maternity and the History of Emotions*, I will show how medieval theologians sundered Mary from the conditions of her womanly sin. They defined her virginity and in so doing articulated what virginity meant in terms of a physical state, and a spiritual situation. They freed her from labour pains, while explaining the theological necessity for the usual difficulties of bearing a child. And eventually, and very controversially, they decided that Mary had never actually been in sin at all. She was clean. Of course, then, we also find out what it means to be dirty according to scholastic theologians. Mary may be less visible, but does her femininity still obtain? I feel like it does.

1 Shame

> As the Fall happened in both sexes, that is, began in the woman and was then completed in the man, so it would be in the reparation. The woman, by believing and conceiving, would begin to conquer the devil in secret, and later her Son would conquer him openly in a duel, that is, on the tree of the Cross. (Gambero 2005, 210)

So wrote the theologian Bonaventure in the thirteenth century. Mary was necessary, he argued, to offer a symmetrical response to Eve's sin. Adam and Eve both fell into sin and both were expelled from the garden. But Eve began the process. Mary, therefore, was required to start the work of repair. Mary's work in doing so was secret; to her son was given the honour of the duel. In this economy, drawing upon a moral calculus devised by Peter Lombard upon whose work Bonaventure was commenting, Eve's sin was pathological while Adam's was accidental. A century or so before Bonaventure, Lombard had argued that Eve's failure was greater than that of Adam because of her hubris. On the one hand, both had sinned; Lombard wrote, 'we say that their pride was equal in making excuses for their sin, and also in eating from the forbidden tree'. On the other hand, only Eve had been contumacious enough and bold enough to decide upon rebellion, to insist on her autonomous will, 'but it [pride] was unequal and much greater in the woman, in that she believed and willed to be like God, which the man did not do' (Lombard 2009, 101). Prior to the creation of Eve, Adam had been told in no uncertain terms that he could have anything he desired except for the freedom to explore good and evil. The book of Genesis implies that Adam had shared this edict from God with Eve: when the serpent approaches her, she tells the creature that she will surely die if she consumes the fruit of the Tree of Knowledge. The serpent, correctly as it turns out, informs her that she will not die. The serpent also tells her, and in this his prediction turns out to be wrong, that should she ingest the fruit she will become like God in that she will have apprehension of the truth that is knowledge of good and evil. Eve is apparently satisfied by the serpent's promises and convinces her husband to join her in the repast.

Adam and Eve are both punished, of course, for their crime. They are both exiled from the garden and are brought into a world of alienation and shame. It is such a stark moment in the Genesis account. Adam and Eve eat the fruit and are suddenly astonished and devastated to notice their own nakedness. Prior to the Fall, Genesis tells us of Adam and Eve that 'they were both naked: to wit, Adam and his wife, and were not ashamed' (Genesis 2:25). But suddenly, this blithe life of the body is rendered impossible. Adam and Eve set to work covering their bodies and concealing themselves from each other and from God. The garden had been a place of integration and safety, putatively free from domination and cruelty. There had been only one condition of this harmony, submission to a Sovereign God, a condition that was violated by Eve's will and Adam's acquiescence to it. For their breach, God inaugurates them into economies of labour and suffering, enmity and pain. Eve, however, is allotted a special additional gendered punishment, according to Genesis, "To the woman also he said: I will multiply thy sorrows, and thy conceptions: in sorrow thou shalt bring forth children, and thou shalt be under thy husband's power, and he shall have dominion over thee" (Genesis 3:16).

Everybody suffers after the Fall, but women must suffer especially. They must suffer the ravages of reproduction, and they must submit to the order of patriarchy. The body of a woman, then, bears sin in a different way to that of a man. The life-giving capacities of a female body are then always also a sign of Eve's fundamental failure, a visible location of shame. They were not ashamed, and then they were. And one of the markers of this shame, given to women alone, is to suffer through childbirth and submit to their husbands. And as we have seen, Aquinas was very keen to make explicit what he thought was implicit in Genesis, the loss of 'virginal integrity' was integral to the shame born by women in this punitive economy.

This is why, according to scholastic theologians, Mary had to be very very special to overcome Eve's devastating work. Mary's purity, theologically, was understood and defined against Eve's transgressions. Where Eve had been proud, Mary was humble. Where Eve had been foolish, Mary was wise. Where Eve had been cunning, Mary was innocent. And where Eve's body was punitively sexed, Mary's body was perennially virginal. With this degree of specialness demanded of Mary, she needed to do women's work of reproduction without participating in any of its punishments. And so Mary is the Virgin Mary. Her sexual purity is required to ameliorate the work of Eve. Her virginity is understood to work in dialectical opposition to the myriad failings of Eve.

Virginity, it would seem, hedges against pride, wilfulness, curiosity and disobedience. Most importantly, virginity stands in opposition to shame. Albert the Great wrote in the thirteenth century that we should 'Behold, "the Mother of Jesus", Mother immaculate, Mother untouched, Mother who never experienced the pains of motherhood, Mother uncorrupt, Mother not deprived of the virtue of virginal chastity' (Gambero 2005, 226). Absolute sexual purity then, purity unavailable to any other woman who gives birth, is what is required to overcome the shamefulness of being a woman.

To be without shame would seem to be the most extraordinary of gifts, to be properly free. This is the normative psychology of the West; we have some notion of shame as damaging, that it (whatever it is) makes us feel bad even though we are not. Sure, our shame responses can help us understand who we are, to encounter our historical traumas and bring them and their shame responses to light. But we are not to trust shame's insistence that there is something rotten at our core; we are to work through shame's work and experience ourselves as without sin. We are also to resist its work when it is deployed by the powerful; we are not to be 'slut shamed' or 'fat shamed'. The idea that shaming is an act of aggression is easily mocked, given the novelty of the usage and the wildness with which the accusation can be thrown around. But the apprehension at the heart of this new use of shaming is a helpful one; it lays bare shame's cultural nature. We can only be slut shamed if the accusation of sluttery lands at a visceral level, but it will only land if we have been inculcated to feel that being a slut is bad. My adipose tissue is exactly that, but the meanings it carries to me and to the world are much bigger (pardon the pun) than my body. The tissue exists as it is, happily and non-harmfully it seems, but the shame accretes in me and leaves me trembling and illegitimate. In this case, the shame is where the policing of women's bodies meets the being in body itself.

A great deal of work has been done in affect theory to theorise shame, much of it building upon Tomkins' argument that shame constitutes one of the basic affects, and it is one 'of indignity, of defeat, of transgression, and of alienation' (Tomkins 1963, 118). Shame, within this definition, comes to the sentient self as a deep awareness that one has sought attachment – to a person, an ideal, a task, a community – and that the attachment has failed because of the incapacity of the self to meet its demands. Shame is friendly with guilt and embarrassment, but it works more profoundly than those feelings because it floods the self so acutely as to feel as though it cannibalises the whole being. Within this framework, shame is prior to cognition, and even to emotions; it works without us knowing why and is irresistible. This telling of shame, articulated most influentially by Eve Kosofsky Sedgwick, has been deployed by affect theorists to argue that shame 'is the place where the *question* of identity arises most originarily and most relationally' (Sedgwick 2003, 37, emphasis in original). That is, shame constitutes a particularly privileged affect, one that is original to the self, and yet embedded in attachment. This use of 'originarily' is striking, positing shame as that which communicates origins, as well as being embedded in the act of being, and refracted through becoming. This claim lies, I think, at the heart of certain critiques levelled against affect theorists, that in arguing for shame's primordial liquidity, they reinstate a nature/culture binary in which shame is somehow prior to the world of culture to which we are subject, and in which our subjectivity emerges. Ruth Leys, for example, has argued that the effect of affect theory, in its Sedgwickian mode, 'is to replace the idea of one's intentions with regard to objects or of the meanings those objects might have for one with the idea of the singularity of one's affective experiences, which is to say with the idea of one's differences from all other subjects' (Leys 2011, 465). Leys point is well taken; some accounts of shame risk divesting it from its location in space, time and history. But where she sees differentiation and individuation as the cost of affect theory, I see its effect in what it offers in terms of relationality. If shame is an affect of transgression and alienation, then in encountering shame we encounter the world or relationality. We transgress something; we are alienated from something. Shame does not shut us off from the world; it is one of the ways we come to make sense of our place within it.

In Christian theology, shame just is, and it is not to be abjured or denied. It is what it is to be. Shame is, according to scholastic theologians, the genetic inheritance of the Fall. That is, all of us born through acts of concupiscence bear original sin. The original sin, that of Adam and Eve, still endures today, seminally distributed through sexual intercourse. I am sure the Church has a raft of new explanations for how original sin is transmitted when children are conceived through in vitro fertilisation, presumably the test tube cannot break the Fall. The shame engendered by original sin is understood to be profound and painful, but it is also constitutive of being human in history itself. Shame is not to be transcended or disavowed. It is, in fact, at the core of what it is to be human in a Christian anthropology: shame offers the space where we might encounter our brokenness, dwell in our relational humanity, and hedge against the false consciousness and spiritual alienation engendered by pride. Virginia Burrus argues that for the early Christians, shame was a modality of ecstasy, a humble space of encounter and transformation, 'offering the generative power of an excessive self-humbling generative encounter that offers in exchange for the sacrifice of face a joyous opening of the subject within grace' (Burrus 2008, 8). Shame was not just what early Christians felt; it was something they used. Shame is a feeling, but it is also a tool. When the *New Catholic Encyclopedia* tells us that 'shame is an alienating affect in which the sharp awareness that the self is somewhat deficient as a human being affects how one lives and operates', this only means that the self is deficient as selves necessarily are after the Fall (New Catholic Encyclopedia 2013, 1415) This theological shame is experienced prior to the cognitive; it is a deep wrenching awareness of brokenness, held in the body as a stored epigenetic trauma that goes all the way back to the book of Genesis. Shame is not personal in a Christian world; it is what it is and obtains for all. But does it obtain differently for women, given that their punishment was gendered? The efforts made by medieval theologians to shield Mary from all aspects of womanly shame would suggest that it was given to women to be more shameful. Mary's virginity is so significant because not only did it protect her from the ordinary desire that accompanies sexual experience, her ontological virginity was held to protect her from original sin itself, from shame.

Debates raged throughout the Middle Ages as to whether Mary herself was the product of an Immaculate Conception, as was her son. That is, theologians wanted to know whether she was conceived and born in a state of grace and free from original sin, or whether God lifted the burden of shame from her at some point in her existence. This particular argument, and its stakes, will be explored in Section 3 of this Element. But whether or not theologians argued for the Immaculate Conception of Mary, they all agreed that her sanctified and peerless virginity represented the absence of shame. The work of Aquinas et al. is crucial to understanding the purchase gained, and which remains, by the articulation of Mary's virginity. Prior to the emergence of the scholastic project, Mary had been represented in the West in complicated and contradictory ways. There was no stable theology of Mary; her perfection had not yet been codified into doctrine. Her cult was popular and somewhat organic. She was thought to be able to intervene in any situation, to perform miracles at the drop of her veil. Elaborate and nasty stories emerged over the course of the Middle Ages that had her protecting innocent Christian children against Jewish enemies. In popular Christian imagination, she was all conquering, and her chastity was that of a belletrix, a womanly warrior, rather than that of a demure maiden. Scholastic theologians argued for a much more stable Mary, one who was ossified by her perfection. Popular Mary was volatile and too easily attached to political volatilities and secular causes. Scholastic theology, which explicitly articulated doctrine from 'authority', drew upon the gospels and the writing of the church fathers, proffering instead a bounded and completed Mary.

Scholastic Mary is luminously beautiful. She is to be adored and emulated. These theologians think about her within the formal categories offered by scholastic thought, using her to think about broader theological issues, but their appreciation tends to the sensual as well. Given the formality of medieval theology, which did not tend to the poetic or the ludic, it is striking to encounter the linguistic pleasure they take in describing her. They take much recourse to the superlative when it comes to the Blessed Virgin. The thirteenth-century theologian Conrad of Saxony, for example, used the erotic language of the Song of Songs to portray Mary's glory. He describes how 'her luminous virginity was excellent, both in her flesh and in her mind. Moreover, in her virginity there was an excellent and luminous fruitfulness: in that fruitfulness was located an excellent and luminous uniqueness' (Gambero 2005, 218). Conrad embarrasses himself with adjectives. Mary is the most of everything good, and in cosmic unity with the world. This was the Mary produced by scholastic theologians over the course of the Middle Ages, a type of spiritual pin-up girl upon whom they could squander their metaphors and cordon her off from the messy world of beings in sin.

Mary is not who she was in the cultural imagination of Western modernity; to non-Catholics, her veneration seems absurd. And yet the idea that womanly virginity and purity are synonymous still holds in very visible ways, as does its location in the language of shame and shaming. See, for example, the example of the purity ring. In the 1990s, in the United States, evangelical leaders started what they called a 'purity movement', designed to encourage young Christians to embrace and declare virginity positively and demonstrably. The ring was worn as a sign of that commitment, a pledge between self and world to keep oneself unviolated. A number of tween, teen and young adult celebrities rode the wave. Selena Gomez, Miley Cyrus and the Jonas Brothers were all proud wearers of this spiritually stain-free jewellery. These stars, all of whom were appearing on their own shows on the Disney network, declared publicly the vow they had made to resist the pressures of a sexually demanding society. In 2008, aged 16, Cyrus declared to *People* magazine that 'Even at my age, a lot of girls are starting to fall' (Orloff 2008). This was the fear that drove the purity movement, that of a fall. A fall into what? Is it a slip or a jump? Can you trip? The theology of the purity ring implied that the border between virtue and vice, safety and sin, was so fine that constant vigilance was required. One could fall into impurity by default, so went the logic; thus, it was necessary to bind oneself to purity with an act of will. And the burden of this virginity fell upon young women particularly; their integrity was more necessary, more epistemologically and spiritually laden than that of young men. As Linda Kay Klein explains it, 'in the evangelical community, an "impure" girl or woman isn't just seen as damaged; she's considered dangerous … For if our men – the heads of our households and the leaders of our churches – fell, we all fell' (Klein 2018, 4).

The Christian industrial complex swung into gear in the era of the purity movement. Purity ceremonies took place at purity balls. Jewellers produced myriad designs for the rings, engraved with biblical quotes, or sometimes with the oft-heard maxim 'true love waits'. Folded into a number of these ritual practices were the affirmation of the relationship between father and daughter. The father escorts the daughter to the ball, and he pledges to help her protect her virginity. The father declares

> I, (daughter's name)'s Father, choose before God to cover my daughter as her authority and protection in the area of purity. I will be pure in my own life as a man, husband and father. I will be a man of integrity and accountability as I lead, guide and pray over my daughter and my family as the high priest in my home. This covering will be used by God to influence generations to come. (Thompson 2007 , p. 297)

The father offers coverage, which will be used by God. The father is the high priest, protecting his home. God, father and home are merged into a space of protection, a safe locus for the virgin's purity to flourish. But in this place, the virgin's intactness must invariably be fetishized. Her unpenetrated vagina becomes the key performance indicator against which the 'high priest' can be judged. If the paterfamilias is transformed into clergy by the task of protecting his daughter, then his priesthood must be measured against its *raison d'être*, which is the containment of the daughter. How is this linked to shame? I might cringe at the gender politics of this purity ball, but why should it correlate with shame? How would we presume to know? If shame is as liquid and surprising and diffuse as affect theory suggests, how can we attach the purity ball, for example, to shame. My provisional answer comes from the movement's self-styled survivors, many of whom collect under the hashtag #noshamemovement. They argue that shame is weaponised by the purity movement to freight women's desire with meanings and responsibilities it cannot, and should not, bear. Michael Warner tells us that shame is everywhere, but also that there are significant 'inequalities of shame' that seek to punish some more others (Warner 1999, 12). Young women in the purity movement are asked to bear more shame for the Christian common good, to avoid the fall described by Miley Cyrus so as to protect the entire community.

Miley's use of the word 'fall' to describe the loss of virginity makes sense. In Latin, the word for 'fall' is *lapsus*. Life in the Garden of Eden, as we have seen, was prelapsarian; Adam and Eve were unalienated and complete. They enjoyed the natural world, and each other, blithely. They were not split into ego, id and superego. They did not experience cognitive or emotional dissonance. But they made a mistake. Their *lapsus*, their slip or error, dragged us all into sin, condemned to the shame of sexed bodies and painful differentiation from God. This is why Miley Cyrus worried, in 2008, about her contemporaries falling. With the loss of their virginity, however naively it may have occurred, Miley's friends had stumbled into postlapsarian brokenness, even though they were already technically fallen there as Christians born in original sin. There is no going back from this mistake, except by the herculean saving efforts of Christ. Simpler, surely, not to go there at all. This is not to say that the pleasures of the flesh are denied to the virgin within this economy, but she must wait until it is vouchsafed by the blessing of marriage, which offsets the sexual sin against the procreative imperative.

There is a logic to the purity movement that transcends its own theology. In popular culture, the loss of virginity is also freighted with heavy significance. In Amy Heckerling's 1995 movie *Clueless*, the heroine Cher is insulted in the cruellest of ways by one of her high school classmates (Clueless 1995). Cher, the queen bee of her Beverly Hills high school, has been working hard to make over Tai, a young woman who has recently moved to Los Angeles. Cher has the body, clothes and money that enable her to flourish at the school. Tai, on the other hand, presents as a rustic ugly duckling needing Cher's sophisticated guidance. But Tai has a different sort of sophistication, alluding to past drug use and sexual competency that leaves Cher in the shade. When this Pygmalion relationship sours, as it inevitably must, Tai asserts her own authority with her riposte to Cher. She looks her squarely in the eyes and says, 'You're a virgin who can't drive.' Cher, recoiling, responds with the immortal line, 'That was way harsh Tai.' And harsh it is. Cher is the self-styled queen of Los Angeles, a city built on cars and sexualisation. Los Angeles's modernity is that of freeways and Hollywood, its leitmotifs are traffic jams and Marilyn Monroe. To be a citizen of this town, Tai suggests, requires adult sexuality and a driver's licence. Cher has the mansion, the face and the extraordinary closet of clothes. But she is a child, condemned to be so until she passes the driving test and loses her virginity. In our post-Freudian modernity, we have decided that sexual expression is crucial to full personhood. If the purity ball is designed to keep the virgin inside the threshold, much of secular culture is promising that adulthood can only occur when the threshold is crossed.

As a child, I felt completely caught between these two ideas of virginity, its double meanings reifying further virginity's importance. Virginity was celebrated in my family and in my Catholic school. It was celebrated theologically, as a state of innocence that protected the young woman from the predations of men, as well as a device to protect them from the shameful state of premarital pregnancy. We were told often that once it is gone, it is gone. There can be no going back. What about confession, we would ask the teachers, surely if we make a mistake we can be forgiven? They would reply that of course we could be forgiven, but our virginity could not be restored. They said, imagine having to tell your future husband that you were not a virgin. Imagine wearing white at your wedding and knowing it was a lie. And in what passed for sex education, a topic that was taught in health classes and named 'family life', we were reminded that illicit sex not only imperilled our souls and threatened to upset our future wholesome husband but also risked the conception of a baby. There is only one of form of contraception that is 100 per cent effective, we were often told. The teachers delivered this statement with the rhythm of a comedian, but it was no joke. The punchline was that abstinence was the only way. My school talked a big game about a myriad of ethical issues, and the school prided itself on teaching social justice to the girls. But it was always clear that there was one breach that would sunder us from our Catholic community in which we lived, and it was not fraud or burglary or animal cruelty or whatever. It was, of course, giving it away before marriage. I once had a teacher at my school who described a character in a novel as a 'nasty little tart who shared herself around'. What a world, in which the worst thing a woman could be was someone who shared herself.

And yet, the promised adulthood afforded by losing it was completely compelling. From the time I was quite little, I had surreptitiously scoured the pages of *Cosmopolitan* magazine at the public library. This was the 1980s and *Cosmopolitan* was rude and exciting. There were sealed sections to be unsealed, and within those pages was so much detail about how to do it, and what doing it might achieve. The object of a flourishing sexual life, or at least this is what I took from those glossy salacious pages, was power. This was a complicated, in fact, contradictory vision of power. But it was power nonetheless. In becoming sexually competent, a young woman could manage men, make use of them and turn their predations to their own benefit. They could, in short, become capital rather than labour. But this was not to be won easily. Armour was required; the accoutrements that guaranteed sexual power needed to adopted. This injunction to sexiness meant what you might expect, an appropriate body girded in the right clothes, painted with make-up, and a topped with a massive mane of hair. I read the magazines and shivered at the possibilities. *Cosmopolitan* presented possibilities of a consuming female carnality, within which sexual desirability and competency were the gateway to being in the world, and mastering it. This carnality was powerful, in that it was designed to bring men to their knees, turning them into humble supplicants. Of course, as I got older, I understood that this was an ideology as punishing as that offered by the fetishization of Mary's maidenhood. Both stories, and I know how rudimentary this insight is, accorded value to a woman on the basis of her sexual availability to men. But, at least to this young woman reading in secret at the Balwyn library in suburban Melbourne, the woman in the magazines turned me on. The same could not be said of the Virgin.

The librarian busted me reading *Cosmo* at the library. She told me that it was not appropriate reading for a young girl. She told my mother. This led to a conversation at home which still makes me blush to recall and arouses deep shame. My parents sat me down and explained to me that sex was beautiful and God-given and something to be cherished and treasured. As such, it deserved and warranted the protection of marriage. Their words reflected those of the Catholic catechism, which declares, 'In marriage the physical intimacy of the spouses becomes a sign and a pledge of spiritual communion.' My parents thought that *Cosmopolitan* suggested that sex was no big deal, that it was just a pleasurable activity akin to eating a nice meal or taking a holiday. Mum and Dad were wrong about that. They were right that these magazines refused to sacralise sex, but the breathy sealed articles about sexual positions, orgasms and seduction made sex a very big deal indeed. They made it all about power and commodification. The commercial culture that was everywhere in my childhood, and much more pervasive than that of the Church, told me that sex was one's passport to authority. And this version of sex was available if I submitted to capitalism's gendered expectations. I needed to objectify myself, to produce myself as sexual specimen, to access full womanly adulthood. In 1988, Cindy Crawford, the supermodel of the era, looked at us directly from the cover of *Cosmopolitan*. She stared aggressively at the viewer, haloed by her wind-machine-blown hair, and the headline read 'What You Can Teach A Man About Sex'(Cosmopolitan 1988).

All of this is to say that virginity meant, and still matters, an awful lot. It is something to be protected or it is something to be happily jettisoned. It is always gendered in that a woman's virginity is more valuable than that of the man – it can do more cultural work. Virginity is considered to be a real physical state, as well as indicating an intangible essence of innocence. Once gone, apparently, virginity is lost forever. The ex-virgin, having 'fallen', is now implicated in the messy pleasures of adulthood, becoming a full psychic citizen, suddenly alert to the complexity and shames of human relationships. Virginity cannot be restored. So what is this thing which is lost? According to Maureen Lauder, writing in the *Encyclopedia of Sex and Gender*, 'virginity is a state of sexual inexperience, and the term is most often used to denote the status of a person – male or female – who has not had penetrative vaginal intercourse' (Malti-Douglas 2007, 291). This is a great definition, in as much as Lauder focuses less upon virginity as a physical reality than on the work that the term does in conferring status. She then goes on to map the ways in which virginity has been understood in different times, locations and cultures. She also notes that the work of LGBTIQ+ activists and scholars in recent times has troubled and challenged the normative aggregation of the idea of virginity and the penetration of a vagina. Lauder's synthesis draws upon significant work in anthropology, psychoanalysis and cultural history that has argued for virginity's enduring social and economic power. Virginity works, of course, at the deep levels of ideology to encode ideas of female purity and desirability. It also works economically to guarantee the efficacy of marriage as mode to peacemaking, social reproduction, and financial consolidation. Marriage has mostly been, in the West at least, a means to secure alliances, navigate political fractures and consolidate communities. The virginity of the bride has been understood to be crucial to ensure the genetic legitimacy of potential offspring, hence the cliché of courtiers in pre-modern societies scouring postnuptial bed linen for the blood that signals the breaking of the hymen. Freud famously outlined much of this history in *The Taboo of Virginity* (Freud 2007). This encyclopedia entry on virginity condenses these myriad ideas and histories of virginity expertly, revealing virginity in its imaginary and putatively biological contexts.

What I find especially striking about Lauder's entry, however, is what follows directly afterwards. The text suggests, for the reader interested in finding out more about virginity, that they should '**See Also** Chastity; Mary, Mother of Jesus' (Malti-Douglas 2007, 294). This small little bit of cross-referencing is suggestive of Mary's role in the making of the concept. She is not just the world's most famous virgin; rather, she is constitutive of virginity. The idea of Mary is essential to what we think virginity means, to the sacredness and the symbolic power the virgin's purity is thought to bear. And this is not just a phenomenon of the Middle Ages. In the history of Western thought, the Reformation is assumed to have done away with the worst excesses of Marian piety, but the necessity of her virginity still obtains in the words of the reformers, and in our own contemporary Christian cultures. Yes, Protestant reformers were scandalised by the array of devotional practices offered to Mary across the European continent, which they argued were idolatrous in that they worshipped Mary as a God, rather than venerated her as was suitable. For example, the sixteenth-century reformer Melanchthon wrote that 'the fact of the matter is that in popular estimation the blessed virgin has replaced Christ. People have invoked her, trusted in her mercy, and sought to appease Christ' (Tappest 1959, 232–3). Reformers also critiqued the lavishness of celebrations of Mary. In answer to the question of how it was appropriate to praise Mary, Melanchthon's contemporary Zwingli said 'not with elaborate and high (church) buildings, with processions where canons ride on beautiful horses, and dine with fine ladies'. He suggested instead that these resources should be deployed 'for the welfare of poor daughters and women, whose beauty is endangered by poverty' (Boss 2007, 317). Marian rituals such as these examples of both theological and material excess appalled reformers. Devotions that celebrated Mary's capacity to mediate between man and God, that implored her to intercede on behalf of the believer, were neither ethical nor scripturally derived. It is these types of criticisms, this refusal of a popularly constructed divinised Mary, that the reformers offered in relation to Mary. But, of course, the great majority maintained the idea of her perpetual virginity. That part of the Mary story was never in doubt.

And so female virginity continued to obtain in the West as a synonym for purity. Reformers used the cult of Mary to make their modernity. The cult of Mary, they argued, reflected everything that was wrong with Catholic excess and corruption. As the Protestant theologian Karl Barth noted in the nineteenth century, 'In the doctrine and worship of Mary there is disclosed the one heresy of the Roman Catholic Church which discloses all the rest' (Beattie 2002 182). From scant scriptural evidence, the reformers argued, Mary had been transformed into a type of Goddess and was worshipped with idolatrous excess. She became a symbol of what was wrong with the past, evidence of the corruptions of the Church. But the reformers had no quibble with celebrating her purity and continuing to enshrine the absolute perfection she received as a result of God's grace. She remained *sui generis*, a model of perfect womanhood which no woman could possibly emulate. The reformers, of course, were bracing and radical in their critique of Catholic ideals of celibacy, particularly in relation to religious communities. They renegotiated Catholic theologies of marriage, which had understood the sacrament as sociologically and demographically necessary, but always spiritually subordinate to the ideal of chastity. Reformers, instead, argued that ostensibly celibate religious communities afforded devastating opportunities for sin. Part of this critique was contextual; Luther and others noted the myriad examples of extramarital sexual activities by so-called celibates, which made a mockery of sacred ideals of chastity. Celibacy also engendered pride, with its adherents claiming a superior spiritual status over married Christians. In a fallen world, in which all believers must surrender to God's absolute power over salvation, reformers saw a focus upon a celibacy as a form of fetish, a fantasy that one could save oneself through works. If sexual shame was a result of the Fall, if it was so fundamental to being human, then a theological fantasy of celibacy was an arrogant refusal of God's punishment.

The Christian family becomes, within this theology, central to spiritual formation and the maintenance of a rigorous Christian life. A faithful marriage, in both senses of the word, becomes an imperative. This is a marriage of spiritual equals, but following Genesis the woman must be subordinate to the headship of her husband. This idea of the family, which radically supplants the ecclesiastical and monastic structures of Catholicism, depends on the dialectic between Eve and Mary just as strongly as did medieval Catholic theology. Eve's failures justify the necessity of womanly submission to the husband, as well as their suffering in childbirth. Mary's virginity models the maidenly virtue that women must bring to their marriages, as well as the docile motherhood to which they should aspire. This returns us to the purity ring ceremony of the twenty-first century, in which the father asserts himself as priest of his family. Protestant reformers replaced the monastery with the family as the primary place of protection and spiritual formation. In so doing, they elevated the father to priest who bore the responsibility for ensuring the purity of the women in his care. They rejected the dogma of Mary but maintained rigorously the ideas of feminine suffering and virtue for which she stood. They held on, happily, to the regimes of gendered shame that Catholic theology had bequeathed to them.

The Catholic Church modernised itself in the nineteenth century, borrowing from the Protestant playbook to develop its own theology of the family. The Church created its own set of family values as it sought to negotiate the challenges of liberalism, capitalism and socialism, as they saw them. Leo XIII's famous encyclical *Novarum Rerum* of 1891 surveyed the perils of the time and argued that individualism and capitalism in particular imperilled souls, both in as much as they created false idols and also that their modes of bodily exploitation impinged upon the capacity of hard-working Catholics to practice their faith. The Pope took aim, also, at revolutionary movements that sought to destroy the established order of things. They refused the sovereignty of God. In answer, the Pope asserted the rights of the family, deploying medieval scholastic theology to do so. The encyclical reads as follows:

> Paternal authority can be neither abolished nor absorbed by the State; for it has the same source as human life itself. 'The child belongs to the father', and is, as it were, the continuation of the father's personality; and speaking strictly, the child takes its place in civil society, not of its own right, but in its quality as member of the family in which it is born. And for the very reason that 'the child belongs to the father', it is as St. Thomas Aquinas says, 'before it attains the use of free will, under the power and the charge of its parents'. (Leo XIII 1891)

Genealogically, this account of the family erases the mother; the child is a continuation of the father's personality. Theologically speaking, this assignation means that the child's biological and social identity continues that of the father. The mother, then, is a vessel of carriage, rather than an active participant in the creation of the child. Of course, the nineteenth century had a much better grasp on human reproduction than the quote implies. But it refracts a Marian theology that argues that the best mother is one who was not involved in the conception of their child. This privileging of the father, as inseminator and as public head of the family, also enshrines the private sphere of the home within which the mother can be consigned. Elsewhere in the encyclical the Pope noted that 'a woman is by nature suited to homework, and it is that which is best adapted at once to preserve her modesty and promote the good bringing up of children and the well-being of the family' (Leo XIII 1891). That sex education at my Catholic school was called 'family life' says it all.

Mary is not static, and neither are the meanings afforded by her virginity. In the Middle Ages, her beautiful virginity was defined against and through the essential shame and sinfulness that attached to all concupiscence, particularly that of women. After the Reformation, Mary's virginity attaches differently, to the articulation of the purity that a young woman should bring to the sacred private sphere of her marriage. In marriage, sinful concupiscence can be contained within the vows of the union and policed by the husband who also serves as patriarch of the household. Both approaches situate Mary's virginity typologically, as remedy for and solution to Eve's excess. Does Mary's virginity have to be figured in this way? Does it have generative feminist theological possibilities? Luce Irigaray suggested that Mary's virginity could do otherwise. She wrote of Mary's encounter with the angel, in which he delivers the news to Mary that she is pregnant with God's baby, that 'the woman-mother of this advent was innocent of the laws, specifically the laws of love. Had no knowledge of the imperatives of desire' (Beattie 2002, 125). Irigaray's Mary is primordial and precedes prior to the law, unmarked by language, 'innocent'. Rather than being a vessel for the logos, and in so doing made victim to its governing logic, she is separated from it, elevated beyond it, of somewhere and something else. This Mary is 'outside any conjugal institution. Was not marked by the language of a father-husband. A virgin in the eyes of the traditional order . . . . That might perhaps give birth to a new figure of history? Arriving from beyond the sky, by mediation of an angel?' (Beattie 2002, 125). But this Mary, to my mind, is old wine in a new bottle. The premium remains upon her purity, her status as unmarked and unviolated. In this telling, there is a place before shame, and the virgin inhabits it. Yes, Irigaray recognises that Mary's virginity was assigned by the traditional order of her time, relativising the concept somewhat. But her overall formulation postulates her innocence and her ignorance as the source of her authority. This Mary can birth a new figure of history because she is outside of history, unmarked by the father/husband.

I think a more helpful repudiation of virginity comes from Miley Cyrus. This is the Miley who worried about her friends falling in 2008 and pledged to keep herself nice before marriage. In 2019, however, she posted on Instagram that 'Virginity is a Social Construct' (Noel 2019). She is of course not the first to say it, but she is probably the most famous. As a child, my friend Wendy asked her mum what 'virgin' meant and her mother replied that 'it's a made-up word.' We used to laugh hard at this story, positing the mother's embarrassment around sexual matters as a reason for her evasion. But Wendy's mum was right; it is a made-up word (as all words are), and it is a made-up notion. But made-up words and notions do lots of work in the world, emotional, ideological, economic, theological and social work in the world. The adjective 'virgin' is very busy in its labours indeed, particularly as a device that aims to generate shame. Yes, shame as described by affect theory is mercurial in as much as it is constantly surprising in its manifestations, awakened in the body to remind us we are not right for our environment, that we have overreached in fantasising some type of connection in the world. But even at its most mercurial, shame still attaches to objects. The relationship between shame and the things that arouse shame is not random – shame attaches to power. The feeling of shame feels individual and its *modus operandi* is to seek privacy and protection; however, shame does not pertain to the subject alone, it is a measure of their being in the world, and the fact that they are indeed subject to something. The scholastics were agents in a shaming project, proudly so, and their authority has been used explicitly right up until the present day to sustain arguments for the theologically necessary submission of women's sexuality. Less explicitly, their ideas still infuse our world in which virginity is prized, derogated and defined. The shame attached to virginity, as a gendered concept, works to remind the woman that whatever her orientation to sexual feeling might be, it can always be wrong, and she should always be on guard.

2 Pain

Mary's extraordinary virginity made her shameless. It also protected her from the physical pain of childbirth. Mary delivered the saviour in joy, scholastic theologians argued, and she remained *virgo intacta* throughout the whole process. In claiming her virginity *in partu*, which means during the birth, theologians insisted that she remained chaste throughout the process. We are so accustomed to think about virginity as a category that denotes the absence of sexual experience that this idea of a virgin birth seems nonsensical. But since Mary was a perpetual virgin, it was necessary that her body show no signs whatsoever of any sort of penetration, even that of a foetus emerging from her body. We can suppose they were talking about the integrity of the hymen when they argued for her virginity in childbirth, although the scholastics were never quite so unseemly to use the word. Instead, they dwelt in the land of theological kitsch. In the twelfth century, Anthony of Padua wrote, 'as lilies retain their freshness, beauty, and fragrance, even when water washes over them, so Blessed Mary, after giving birth to her Son, retained the freshness and beauty of virginity' (Gambero 2005, 201). It was not possible that Mary could give birth as a normal woman, because that would almost certainly involve pain. Pain in childbirth was a direct punishment from God, afforded to women after the Fall. So Christ's birth was a supernatural event that left Mary fresh as a daisy, which was handy given that she was in a stable.

Pain was very important in Western medieval culture. It was the result of the Fall and so was always linked to the soul. An individual might feel pain for an innocuous reason like falling over or stubbing their toe. But it was always a register of a larger theological fact – that humans had fallen spiritually, and so their lot was to suffer. To be human was to feel pain, because that was in fact the punishment of original sin. The word 'pain', in fact, comes from the Latin *poena,* which means punishment. Theologians understood pain quite broadly; they often yoked together the physical pain felt with a toothache with the psychic pain felt with a betrayal or a loss. They were of a type in that all pain was an example of a self at odds with its world, a body in decay or a mind in confusion. This was not to say that they rejected the physiological basis of pain; they wrote treatises on medicine as well as theology. It is to say, however, that they sought a spiritual solution prior to a medical one. In 1215, the Fourth Lateran Council, about which we will hear much more, advised that a physical ailment should be treated, in the first instance, theologically, that is a physician of the body when called to minister to the sick must 'warn and persuade them first of all to call in physicians of the soul so that after their spiritual health has been seen to they may respond better to medicine for their bodies, for when the cause ceases so does the effect' (Tanner 1990, 245). The Christian body was integrated, in as much as its frailty was always linked to the sin shared by all men. This is not to say that patients became sick due to their own sins; the theory of causality was not so crude, but it was to say that corporeal life owed its health and flourishing to the spiritual order. Pain was a symptom that could be interpreted in the broadest of registers. The first order of diagnosis was to think about the state of the soul; the body came afterwards.

Pain was also futurological. Come the resurrection of the body, those who were saved would assume a perfect physical form, unblemished and healthy. There would be no pain in heaven. Scholars debated at length about just how good our bodies would be in heaven. They mostly agreed, however, that resurrected bodies in heaven would be as they were as if the Fall had not happened, and they would be the same age as that of Christ when he died, around thirty-three years old. The resurrected body in hell, on the other hand, would bring her postlapsarian body with her. She will feel pain acutely and devastatingly, and the torments will last for eternity. And so, the experience of bodily pain, for the Christian believer, could always be a nasty taste of things to come. It presaged the potential of eternal strife and torture, reminding the sufferer of the need for virtue in this life to avoid pain that may come in the afterlife.

Scholastic theology, as I have argued, was a shaming technology. Theologians articulated doctrine, which was made canon law at papal councils that encouraged the faithful to dwell within their shame to achieve spiritual growth. The body was real, and in its desires and its sufferings it offered a world of symptoms that signalled the omnipresence of sin, and the necessity of its overcoming. At the same time, this meant that pain was also universal and standard. There could be no life without pain; it was the cost of doing business. And so theology also enabled pain to be an agent of self-knowledge, and sometimes of spiritual pleasure (although they would not have called it that). Theologians devoted a great deal of time to different sorts of pains, producing a type of *Diagnostic and Statistical Manual* describing how and what different types of pain signified. As Esther Cohen has it, 'professionals of pain management and interpretation – preachers, scholars, physicians and jurists – told sufferers they could trace their pain back to Eve, the first human who gave birth in pain' (Cohen 2009, 3). Devotional writers, also, went to great lengths to describe their suffering, in expressive and overpowering language. In particular, mystics often imagined themselves with Christ at the crucifixion, bearing his wounds and grieving over his anguish. Most famously, Francis of Assisi identified so profoundly with Christ's suffering that he experienced the stigmata: he developed wounds that matched those of Christ upon his body. The stigmata itself became a devotional technology, proliferating throughout the late Middle Ages upon the bodies of holy men and women.

And pain was a mode to a different sort of truth than that of spiritual rapture; inquisitors instrumentalized it to uncover heresy, via practices of torture. Like Talal Asad, I see the self-imposed pain of mystics as embodying the same logic as that imposed by the torturer; both are 'part of the genealogy of disciplining-the-body-for-getting-at-the truth' (Asad 1983, 247). At the Fourth Lateran Council of 1215, an epochal council for the Church, for the first time it was mandated that all Christians participate in confession once a year. In this moment, Foucault famously recognised what he saw as the codification of the confessing subject in the history of the West. By this, he meant that Lateran IV inscribed a move already emerging in medieval political culture towards privileging the confession as a locus of truth, as opposed to the commonplace reliance upon ordeals and customs for the management of disputes, and the administration of justice. Lateran IV does not only mandate the sacrament of penance, which is the outcome of the confessional process, it also forbids clerical participation in the practice of ordeals. As Robert Bartlett has shown, from the early Middle Ages onwards, a myriad and diverse practice of ordeals had been deployed across Europe to seek truth and resolve conflict. The idea at the heart of the ordeal is that guilt could best be established through divine intervention; whether in a duel or a physical test, God would intervene to offer proof of culpability (Bartlett 1986). Lateran IV forbade clerical participation in these tests, on the basis that it contravened the biblical injunction against tempting the Lord. It was not for humanity to make demands on God in this way. And so at the same time as the ordeal is rejected as a legitimate mode to the truth, confession is established as a mode to epistemological surety, gaining its most secure purchase in inquisitorial procedures that emerged subsequent to 1215. This move, at Lateran IV, 'helped give the confession a central role in the order of civil and religious powers', writes Foucault (Foucault 1978, 58). The confessing subject was, and is, one who contains truth internally. To confess is to yield that truth to an external power. Since medieval theologians had already, by 1215, begun to systematize the relationship between pain and truth in the Christian subject, it should not surprise that their inquisitorial colleagues sought to use pain as a method of truth extraction in the form of torture. Torture was deployed bureaucratically and systematically, as theologians and inquisitors understood it, to uncover the truth through pain.

Scholastic theologians and inquisitors were mostly not the same people, although there was certainly overlap. But scholastic theology produced the orthodoxy that enabled inquisitors to produce heresy. At Lateran IV, the first papal council that was administered by scholastic theologians and organised under the authority of the first scholastically trained pope, the Council declared boldly, 'There is one Universal Church of the faithful, outside of which there is absolutely no salvation', and went on to propagate a striking reform agenda that began with high theology and then moved to the regulation of sacramental life (Tanner 1990, 230). The Council taxonomized orthodoxy, refusing the idea of regional variations and cultural inflections in the practice of faith, instead insisting upon uniformity throughout Christendom. Concomitantly, the Council articulated strict penalties for those in breach and stipulated that local religious authorities conduct forensic investigations of the practices of their communities. Lateran IV authorised bishops to interrogate parishioners about their own practices, and those of their neighbours. The Council also insisted that Jews and Muslims in Christendom must wear distinguishing clothes, so that their difference be clearly manifest. Christendom, as it was defined at Lateran IV, was robustly orthodox, but always at threat from the contamination of perfidy, heresy and apostasy.

So the confessing subject in the history of the West becomes visible as Christendom fantasises itself into unity through the demarcation of the aberrant. The Inquisition begins around the same time as Lateran IV, and the constitutions of that Council are the urtext used to define heresy, and pain is the chief mechanism used to extract it. Because pain was true, in an ontological sense, it was a truth wrangler.

So, what then of pain in childbirth, which is a ubiquitous and scouring form of pain, what type of work could it do in this economy of pain? One would assume that labour pains could be replete with meaning; after all, as Jennifer Glancy has pointed out, 'the reception history of Genesis 3:16 suggests that, through women's physical suffering in childbirth, pain plays a condign role in a divine juridical economy' (Glancy 2010, 87). The surprising answer, however, as to the question of meaning of pain in childbirth, at least among scholastic theologians, is that it did not warrant much discussion. The meaning offered by labour pain was static; it stood for gendered subjection after the Fall and was accepted as such. God had been very explicit that this particular type of pain was a perennial indication of failure. As such, childbirth was not worth mentioning, except in the claim that Mary was spared its ignominies. It is a powerful silence, a more than significant omission. Theologians meditated upon Christ's suffering, as well as that of his mother as she grieved his pain. Devotional art and literature exhorted the believer to encounter their own pain through the crucifixion, to understand their own frailty through that of the incarnate God. This pain could be redemptive and aid in the healing of soul and body. Theological discourse licenced the deployment of pain in the acquisition of truth; it was only right that heretics should suffer to confess their contamination of the body spiritual. The pain imposed by the torturer could also redeem; inquisitors claimed that they sought to aid the heretic to return to the faith, not abjure it. And even if there were no redemption of the individual, it was clear that the pain imposed upon the tortured body would help to redeem communities, to clean them up. But Mary's miraculous virginity *in partu* made the pain of childbirth a thing apart. Labour pain, in this world, was consigned to the realm of female experience. It seems that no meaning could be made of it, except that it represented God's sovereign punishment upon women.

I had not thought much about Mary's virginity *in partu* until I gave birth in 2004, until I laboured. As a pregnant woman I was not thinking of Mary at all. Instead, I pored over triumphant accounts of unmedicated midwife-led births, in which women described a transcendent experience of power and freedom.

These accounts admitted pain, excruciating pain, but extolled the potency of its overcoming, and the joyous satisfaction of its relief upon delivery. They also extolled the negative liberty of a 'natural' birth, freedom from medicalization and unnecessary risky intervention. These accounts were compelling in that they offered meaning through pain, in terms of both personal satisfaction and the repudiation of birth as medical pathology. So, with my partner, I strove for and imagined myself into such a birth. There was nothing to fear, the midwife said at one of the appointments, except for fear itself. And since I was giving birth in the United States, which at that time had a far higher rate of elective caesarean births and infant mortality than did my home country Australia, my anxiety about excessive medicalization made, and still does, good sense. When I had my second child in 2010 in a public hospital in Australia, the prenatal care was shared between midwives and obstetricians. Together they assessed my case, and the plan for the birth was negotiated by all of us. In Baltimore in 2004, however, I did not have that option. I had to choose either a midwife or obstetrician/gynaecologist. The midwife option seemed to be the more rational choice, offering a confident approach to birth that embodied feminist principles. And so that is what I did. I did the classes, wrote the birth plan, and we set off to the hospital full of excitement.

Of course, nothing went to plan. The experience cannot be written. For me, Elaine Scarry is exactly right when she says, 'Whatever pain achieves, it achieves in part through its unsharability, and it ensures this unsharability through its resistance to language' (Scarry 1985, 4). During Honora's birth, I crossed over into pain's ontology; it is its own world and for its duration I was obliterated. I must stress, as the ashen-faced midwife did afterwards, that this was an unusually difficult birth. I suffered a fourth-degree tear, which means that I tore from sphincter to vagina. After Honora emerged, I was taken to an operating theatre for repair under general anaesthesia. There was no post-partum mother-daughter bonding, no skin to skin as they call it now. Instead of the exhilaration I had so hopefully forecast, I was mute and shredded. My point in recounting the dazzling stories of triumphant births that had fed my imagination during my pregnancy is not to trouble or mock the experiences of those women. While everyone is born, births vary enormously. But my particular birthing story is one of abject horror, and the destruction of self. In the pain, I could find no bridge to anything I recognised; there was no familiarity and there was no language. I could not ask for help. In that place, relief seemed impossible. The pain felt like it was my being now and I was outside of time. But, thankfully, time came back and since it was 2004 when I was finally able to try to find some words, all I could think to say was 'Guantanamo Bay.' This was the year of the leaking of the infamous torture memos which had been written to mount legal justifications for the deployment of 'enhanced interrogation techniques' (Cohen 2012). That was where I went after childbirth, straight to torture. Actually, I said something else as well, 'After all the money I've spent on recreational drugs you'd think I might have been a natural for the epidural.' In recounting this story of pain, and that I went straight to torture in my attempt to understand it, I am not trying to draw any equivalence between the two. If it seems glib, I apologise and I accept the criticism. My point is that it was only when I experienced the horrific power of transcendent and obliterating pain that I grasped the essence of the torturer's ambition, to impose devastating pain upon the subject so that they are incapable of holding on to their intentional and strategic self.

As someone who had never been scared of legal or illegal drugs, in the time after the delivery I pondered why I chose to birth the way that I did, why I eschewed pain relief. What was I thinking? I was thinking that it could not possibly be that bad. I had experienced broken bones and other injuries. I had felt quite terrible before, so I thought that I was prepared. And if it was cheaper, kinder and better for mother and baby to keep it as simple as possible, then surely that was the best approach. But I now know that I had not experienced ontological pain before the event. I could not have known, because that type of pain is unknowable. But the other reason I made the choice that I did was that I believed, or was led to believe, that pain in childbirth is not like other pain. As the proponents of natural childbirth will tell you, a pregnant woman is not sick, she is not broken, and her body is doing what it was programmed to do. This is not the same as pain that occurs when you break a leg – that pain is alerting you to a problem, to something that needs fixing. Labour pains are something else entirely; they are a register of the wholesome, the production of new life. As such, this is a powerful pain and a productive pain, one that can be generative. In a recent article in the midwifery journal *Women and Birth*, Laura Whitburn et al. synthesised this position as to the otherness of pain in childbirth:

> If a woman can sustain the belief that her pain is purposeful (i.e. her body working to birth her baby), if she interprets her pain as productive (i.e. taking her through a process to a desired goal) and the birthing environment is safe and supportive, it would be expected that she would experience the pain as a non-threatening, transformative life event. (Whitburn et al. 2019, 34)

I found these ideas compelling at the time of my first pregnancy, the idea that pregnancy and birth should not be made into a problem to be solved, but fully experienced as the extraordinary process that it can be. I have no doubt that all of this has been true for a great many women. But I do not buy that pain in childbirth is constitutively different from other pain because its result is puta-tively joyous. Pain is pain.

My past historicist sceptical self would roll her eyes at such an absolutist statement as pain is pain. Have I fallen into what Joanna Bourke calls the 'ontological fallacy' of reifying pain as an agent (Bourke 2014, 5)? Bourke's criticisms were directed against Scarry who, in *The Body in Pain*, had argued compellingly for pain as that which undoes the self, depriving the subject of their aptitude for using language and situating themselves in time. This deprivation is othering; the sufferer is not able to find herself or reach out to others legibly. She is unmade. Bourke resists this notion of pain as totalising and argues instead that 'crucially, pain is not an intrinsic quality of raw experience, it is a way of perceiving an experience' (Bourke 2014, 7). For Bourke, pain can only be comprehended as a form of perception, a knowledge that humans come to have about themselves and their experiences. I take a great deal of her points. Accounts of pain, the policing of pain, the erotics of pain – these vary enormously across time and place. But even if we follow her logic, that we only encounter pain through its perceptions, surely it is striking that profound pain is so often perceived as ontological. Pain is mystical, in both its horror and its sublimity. Whether or not pain has truth, whether it is a thing, to me seems to be hardly the point. The point is, as Scarry so eloquently describes, that in 'serious pain the claims of the body utterly nullify the claims of the world' (Scarry 1985, 33).

If pain were not able to do this, to nullify the world, then we would not work so hard to manage it. And if pain were not so powerful, it would not be used in torture. Surely, it is possible to dwell with pain as something that feels ontological (and has done so within a great many ontologies), while also appreciating the historicity of its manifestations and management in varying contexts. This is where I turn to affect again, aware of the ahistorical risk I run. Affect theory enables us to encounter those apprehensions that feel irruptive, excessive and uncontainable. This does not mean that those affects evade locution, defy cognitive relations or exist without culture; it is to say that they feel like they do and so they have a tenacious power. Donovan Schaefer has written that affect theory registers 'the reefs that subsist below the level of rational control, linguistic sedimentation, or affective flux but nonetheless shape our encounters with power' (Schaefer 2015, 45). Pain is desperately entirely real and also subject to discursive construction. Pain hurts and is hurtful and this means different things to different people. Affect theory helps us hold this together, with no denial of historicity whatsoever. So if, in making this claim, I have landed in an 'ontological fallacy', I will take it.

It is precisely because of pain's undoing potential that it has such a rich, destructive and diverse history. And this is why the idea that Mary did not suffer in childbirth is so telling, and so erasing. The twelfth-century abbot Philip of

Harvengt was not strictly a scholastic theologian, but as an exegete later theologians would deploy his writings. He wrote at length on the Virgin, and he did so in a way that amplified her perfection by describing the necessary corruption he assigned to all other women. Please excuse the long quote, but I think it is worth it because Philip reads Mary's perfect being and perfect birthing against all other women, who are 'deformed in their maternal likeness':

> Observing her spiritual beauty, the angel said, 'Blessed are you among women: and among all women she is so, in comparison with the rest; she is blessed, compared to those upon a whom a harsh curse was inflicted by Eve's fault and who are conformed to wretched law to Eve, the first sinner, and subjected to sins, deformed in their maternal likeness. Among these others, wretched and deformed, a fuller beauty has been granted to this Virgin, who has overcome the ancient curse and the hereditary law. As the Spirit over-shadowed her, she put away from herself the passion of the wickedness and the stain of sin and set herself up higher than all other by the merits of her innocence and her inner beauty.
>
> She rejoiced in her physical virginity, but that she might become even more beautiful, she was made with child in a totally new and unexpected manner, and in a birth beyond words the Virgin brought forth a Child like no other, such as no woman ever bore, before or since. What is so grand and lofty as the wonderful and eminent beauty of this Virgin? Her beauty not only puts her ahead of other women but makes her by far the most outstanding and beautiful of them all. (Gambero 2005, 183)

Philip makes apparent what the Virgin Mary enables in Christian theology – her freedom from abjection makes all the more monstrous the normal embodied lives of women. All women are wretched and deformed, burdened by Eve's fault. Mary, wonderful and eminent, free from passion, radiates beauty. She gave birth without words, but not because she was broken by pain, but because she was protected from it. She presents here like a radiant supermodel on Instagram who, two weeks post-partum, posts a photo of herself in workout clothes looking as if she had never been pregnant. Mary's painless birth testifies to a refusal, on the part of the Western tradition, to engage with childbirth as a site of pain, and as a profound place of unmaking and making.

I was not scandalised by Mary's pain-free birth until after I gave birth myself. But I thought a lot about it afterwards. I thought about saying the rosary at my grandma's house, when she received the honour of hosting her parish's Fatima statue. The statue went to a different house every week, and the host's task was to welcome the pious of the parish on a nightly basis to recite the prayers, bringing their own rosary beads. Grandma loved it, and so grudgingly I joined her on occasion. My resistance usually wore down, as the praying was some-what hypnotic, even if my emerging critical faculties found the statue a bit tacky. These memories, which had been comforting, were transformed by my own birthing experience. I thought about the women around that statue, my grandma's friends, children of the depression. Their hard lives of labour, both in paid work and in households, were etched on their faces and bodies. Many of them had born and raised a number of children; some of them had lost children at birth too. These women were deeply comforted by praying to Our Lady. She was beautiful to them, and they enjoyed her. I had been glad grandma had Mary; she was nourished by her. But at what cost? What does it mean to be inscribed as wretched and deformed by your faith, and to have the psychic profundity and bodily transformation of birthing denied as a site of significance, except as a register of sin?

Exactly one month to the day after Honora's birth, the Metropolitan Museum of Art announced that it had purchased Duccio's *Madonna* for a cost estimated to be more than forty-five million dollars. This was, at that time, the most expensive purchase in the Met's history. The painting is tiny and depicts a serene Mary with the infant Christ, who is reaching out to touch her face. It is a tender evocation of the natality at the heart of Christianity, the radical idea that God became like us. Philippe de Montebello, the director of the Met, was jubilant about the purchase. He declared, 'The first slide in an art history 101 course is a Duccio .... He was one of the founders of Western Art' (Vogel 2004). Mary is present, then, at another great birth, that of Western Art – another birth at which she was central but impassive, crucially there but inactive and acted upon, this time by the painter. If we make and unmake ourselves through pain, Mary was denied participation in her own making. Freedom from pain may seem to be the ultimate liberation, but for Mary it could be argued to constitute a significant privation.

3 Stain

Mary did not become immaculate, officially, until 1854 when Pius IX issued the papal bull *Ineffabilis Deus*. In the bull, the Pope assigned extraordinary potency to the Virgin: she is 'the all fair and immaculate one who has crushed the poisonous head of the most cruel serpent and brought salvation to the world: in her who is the glory of the prophets and apostles, the honor of the martyrs, the crown and joy of all the saints'. This is Mary as warrior and as fortress. As immaculate, she is able to crush the serpent because she is free of his sinful legacy, untainted by his work. She 'is the most excellent glory, ornament, and impregnable stronghold of the holy Church; in her who has destroyed all heresies and snatched the faithful people and nations from all kinds of direst calamities' (Stanglin 2014, 392). Mary's Immaculate

Conception was now official dogma, although its idea had been debated and celebrated since the early Middle Ages. To be immaculate meant that she was understood to have been conceived without original sin, the only human to be granted what was called her 'privilege'. Throughout the history of Christian theology, she was always considered to have been sanctified, to have been liberated from the stain at some point. But it was another thing altogether to conceive of her conception as immaculate, sundering her from the genetic inheritance that is the lot of humanity. Throughout the Middle Ages, the more normative approach was to argue against the Immaculate Conception, to argue that sin was taken from her at some stage in her life, that she was wiped clean by God as a reward for excellent performance, for executing her key performance indicators. It was only in the late medieval writings of John Duns Scotus that serious scholastic arguments were made for the doctrine of the Immaculate Conception, the idea that she was never defiled in the first place, that she was without stain.

Christian soteriology, the theology of salvation, is understood through temporality. After the Fall, humans were plunged into sin and they were plunged into history. All subsequent humans were to bear the postlapsarian stain in real time. God's integrity depended upon the maintenance of this rule. For the punishment to do its work, there could be no exceptions. The incarnation was an intervention into history from outside; it also took place in real time. From the age of the Mosaic Law, as Paul had it, history moved into the age of the spirit in which the operations of grace made salvation possible. The incarnation did not work retrospectively; it did not enable Abraham or Moses to fast track into heaven after the resurrection. For their bad timing, the heroes of the Hebrew Bible found themselves in *limbo patrum*, the limbo of the fathers. *Limbo patrum* was no hell, but it was no paradise either. They were born on the wrong side of history, and that was that. And so, the suggestion of Mary's Immaculate Conception was a troubling one. What would it mean if God made such an exception; surely it would mean that he could do so for Abraham et al., and if he could do so, why had he not? The other problem was that the stain of original sin applied only to rational creatures – namely, a person constituted by body and soul. How could God remove the stain from someone who did not yet exist? Making Mary immaculate was a theological project fraught with risk, and many scholastic theologians thought it was an unnecessary one. Mary was already pretty special; did she need to be utterly exceptional?

As I wrote the first draft of this Element, the state of New South Wales, in which I live, was placed in a state of emergency. A number of uncontrolled bushfires were burning across the state, and the army was mobilised to aid fire services with logistical support. Sydney was cloaked in smoke. Politicians, and much of the media, were shutting down questions about the relationship between the inferno and climate change. We can talk about this when the crisis is over, they said, but this is not the time. Normal discourse was suspended; we found ourselves in the place of thoughts and prayers. This is an example of the privilege of the exception, which belongs to the sovereign, as famously defined by Carl Schmitt (2005). Sovereignty might seem to prevail through norms, but in fact it is constituted by its capacity to overrule them. The exception lays bare political theology; it reveals the ontological claims to power at the heart of a regime, the real basis of authority being claimed by the sovereign. In the case of these bushfires, the state of emergency foreclosed discussions of the Australian continent as a landmass that has been colonised, cultivated and exploited. Instead, the state authorised itself as the valiant wrangler of nature's inchoate fury, a necessary corrective force in a hostile and vengeful environment. And as I revise this text, months after the bushfires, I am doing so under Covid-19 lockdown, experiencing another state of emergency, this time in response to the crisis of pandemic. The sovereign has again deployed the exception, depriving us of liberties for the purpose of protection and of urgently required sanitation. In normal time in liberal democracies, we are inculcated in a habitus, however fantastic, that claims autonomy and free movement, of meritocracies and mobility. For now, right now, these freedoms have withered overnight, as we live as bounded subjects. The state of emergency, the suspension of normal time, reveals the reality of law in its abrogation.

In a state of emergency, in which rights and duties under the normal order no longer obtain, the sovereign dispenses privileges rather than entitlements. The sovereign grants privileges because he perceives their necessity, not because he ought or is bound to do so. As Alain Boureau has written, 'In common parlance privilege seems the opposite of law; whether attached to individuals or groups, it represents an exemption resulting from an arbitrary decision, new or inherited' (Boureau 2001, 621). This is why the question of Mary's Immaculate Conception was a juridical one, as well as a theological and spiritual problem. Why would God suspend his own law to grant Mary this extraordinary privilege? Theologians worked on decoding laws from their knowledge of God, and then worked to construct doctrine from their apprehension. Such a suspension as that of Mary's Immaculate Conception undermined their whole premise. Although they understood that knowledge of God was always timorous and limited, they were also committed to the order of reason to which they claimed their own privileged access. What if God, himself, was not so committed? Arguments for Mary's perpetual virginity could be made through scripture and were consolidated by the idea that Mary's perfection was necessary to undo Eve's failure. That is, although Mary's perpetual virginity required the supernatural, this was an intervention coherent with Christian temporality. The Immaculate Conception was the opposite; it was a-temporal and therefore constituted an exceptional rupture to the order of things.

The late thirteenth-century theologian John Duns Scotus offered the key argumentative move for the Immaculate Conception and became known for these efforts by the title Marian Doctor. He insisted that 'if the authority of the Church or the authority of Scripture does not contradict such, it seems probable that what is more excellent should be attributed to Mary' (Wolter 2000, 55). This was a striking theological departure from precedent. Scotus was not interested in participating in the florid accounts of Mary's beauty and virtue that had characterised some earlier scholastic accounts of the Virgin. He was not particularly interested in her at all as a historical figure or as a location for devotion. Rather, he conceived of the problem of the Immaculate Conception as one that enabled investigation into the limits of God's power. Surely, he claimed, there are none. Nothing should be impossible for God, and to argue that it was not possible that Mary was conceived without original sin was to risk limiting God. God made the rules, but he was not trapped within them. The key word in his Marian formulation is 'probable'. He was not endorsing the Immaculate Conception as doctrine; he was refusing to rule it out.

The tension around the Immaculate Conception, and God's capacity, refracted other significant debates of the period that pertained to God's power. Scholastic theologians began to theorise, in the thirteenth century, the difference between God's *potentia absoluta* and *potentia ordinata*, absolute and ordained power. These concepts were understood by Scotus juridically, as had been his discussion of the Immaculate Conception. Absolute power is that which enables the holder to act beyond the law, while ordained power is that which grants authority within an established legal order. In God's absolute power, he creates and orders his creation with structuring logics, which are legible in his expressions of his ordained power. Humans could know or glimpse God through these structuring logics, which had been most fully elaborated in scripture, and which continued to reveal themselves after the incarnation through the operations of grace in the world. This was the order of reason to which theologians claimed access; it was the evidence of God's ordained power working in the world. But God's absolute power meant that anything could be otherwise at any given moment. Suspension or obliteration was always possible. The rule of law was entirely contingent upon God's permission and maintenance. God, as sovereign, could decide upon whatever exception he might choose, perhaps even that of Mary's Immaculate Conception.

From my reading, the intellectual context for Scotus's advocacy of the Immaculate Conception must partly be ascribed to these debates about the nature of God's power. But in the scholarship there is the Marian Doctor Scotus and there is the Scotus as philosopher, and they do not meet. In Richard Cross's *Duns Scotus,* which offers a synthetic introduction to the very complicated work of the thinker, Cross has nothing to say about the Immaculate Conception whatsoever (Cross 1999). The same can be said of a number of volumes devoted to Scotus as a philosopher theologian, which detail his metaphysics, cognitive theory, ontology and moral theology. On the other hand, in histories of Marian theology and devotion, the debates over the Immaculate Conception are deployed as a register of Mary's centrality to religious culture but are not considered as integral to the theological project itself. The Scotus who theorised the nature of God's power does not figure here, only his avocation for Mary's stainlessness.

Duns Scotus argued for a Mary's stainlessness to extraordinary effect. And yet his arguments for the Immaculate Conception are not accorded any status as part of his philosophical oeuvre. He, it would seem, has been cleansed too. What is it about Mary that needs to be excised from his record? How is it that Scotus's meditations upon the nature of the incarnation are reckoned the stuff of philosophy, but not his Marian formulations? The *Stanford Encyclopedia of Philosophy* includes Scotus and breaks his thought down into the categories of natural theology, metaphysics, theory of knowledge and ethics and moral psychology (Williams 2019). These were not categories that would have obtained for Scotus. He framed his intellectual commentaries within the normative format of a commentary on Lombard's *Sentences*, the standard pedagogical assignment in medieval theology. It takes detailed work to formulate his ideas along the lines of modern philosophical inquiry, to make his theology into 'Philosophy' with a capital 'P'. The entry is creative exegetical work, which reads a philosophical project into a theological corpus. There is no intellectual reason that the Marian formulation could not be made to fit. Scotus's discussion of Mary could viably be placed into any of those categories had the author sought to do so. So why is she not there? Marilyn McCord Adams has called the Immaculate Conception a 'thought-experiment in medieval philosophical theology' and has shown how it was a ground on which a number of important issues were negotiated over the course of the Middle Ages (Adams 2010). But in contemporary philosophical accounts of Scotus, Mary is almost never allowed in.

There is something embarrassing about Mary, it would seem. Maybe all mothers are just embarrassing. I am certainly embarrassed by my mother on occasion, and my children seem to find me the same way. Perhaps Mary, as mother, embarrasses philosophy. She is too much of a reminder of the fact of being born, of humans as animal. She also reminds philosophy of its own historical contingency: Scotus's investigations into the Immaculate

Conception remind us that thought emerges in particular moments of belief and reflects the imperatives of its time. But Scotus worked so hard to remove her of anything embarrassing that he made her utterly perfect. And yet his Mary is still excluded from his philosophical canon – his mother is silenced. Robyn Ferrell has argued that because maternity is assigned to the natural, it is abhorrent to the practice of philosophy which proudly imagines itself to be denaturalising. For Ferrell, 'no doubt, there is yet no mother theory in philosophy, because these terms are nearly oxymoronic.' Philosophy, she argues, abstracts and extrudes. It does not dwell in the mess of the real; instead, it seeks to distance itself from the squalor of being to practice the art of naming and containing the world through theory, performing proudly 'its most *unnatural* act' (Ferrell 2006, 3–4, emphasis in original). Philosophy's extrusion of a Scotus without mother, a mother to whom he devoted a great deal of devoted thought, speaks to what Ferrell describes. Strangely, perversely, he did develop something of a mother theory, and philosophy has no place for it.

This is not to say his mother theory was adequate to the task. What work did the Immaculate Conception do? Mary becomes immaculate in scholastic theology around the same time that she is being marshalled against impurity, particularly against Jews. The 1854 papal bull makes this work clear and reflects how Mary had come to stand for a perfect Church in the centuries following Scotus's insights, and as the figure who protects Christians from heresy. To reprise *Ineffabilis Deus*, she is the 'impregnable stronghold of the holy Church; in her who has destroyed all heresies and snatched the faithful people and nations from all kinds of direst calamities' (Stanglin 2014, 392). Mary's purity might have been excluded from the philosophical record, but it did great ideological work for the Church in the late Middle Ages and early modernity as it sought to imagine itself anew in the wake of a pluralising religious and economic world. Mary becomes the protagonist in myriad lurid stories in which Christian children are preyed upon by Jews and saved through the miraculous intervention of the Virgin. The most famous of these is Chaucer's *The Prioress's Tale*, in which a young boy was murdered by Jews and left upon a dung heap. His murderers are found and executed for the crime. In spite of his death, the young boy continues to sing a hymn in praise of the Virgin during his requiem mass. He describes how he received a vision from the Virgin who placed a grain on his tongue, and that he will continue to sing until the grain is removed. Once the grain is removed, the boy dies. As Miri Rubin has written, 'As Mary emerged increasingly pure, so her detractors emerged ever more perverse' (Rubin 2004, 9). Or, as Amy Remensnyder notes in her discussion of the role played by Mary in Cervantes's stories of Christian liberation against Muslims in Spain, 'the Virgin offered Christians a symbolic field on which to articulate the nature of their encounters with non-Christians' (Remensnyder 2007, 645). This symbolic field is that of purity.

Mary's virginity already encoded purity, of course. But this was a gendered form of purity. Once she was conceived of as immaculate, her purity could more easily speak for the integrity of the Church, *Ecclesia,* herself. And as the idea of *Ecclesia* came to be more explicitly linked with state formation and articulation as a result of the Reformation, this purity could easily be yoked to the realm of the political and the biological. Although *Ineffabilis Deus* was not proclaimed until 1854, throughout the early modern period the Immaculate Conception was celebrated in liturgy and in devotion. It was doctrine by popular assent, if not in law. Mary immaculate came increasingly to hedge against pollution and corruption, against defiled enemies, be they Jews, Muslims, heretics or reformers. Since Mary Douglas's epochal *Purity and Danger*, published in 1966, scholars have applied her ideas about the relationship between pollution and taboos to a great many places and times. She and others in her wake have argued that our species hedges against instability and flux by producing ideas of the clean against which we can define threats as dirty and potentially contaminating. It is so striking, when we think through clean, that Mary's conception is not named as being without original sin, but that she is without its stain. The word *macula* from which comes the word 'immaculate', in Latin refers primarily to a spot, mark or stain. The verb *maculo* can mean to defile, stain or pollute. Mary's purity was much more than figural; her Immaculate Conception bears connotations of total cleanness, in opposition to dirt and pollution.

Our world is still obsessed by purity, literal and figural. Mary is not the sole maker of this obsession, but her story certainly reflects the work that we imagine clean to do. We want to believe that clean can protect us, that it can build a cordon sanitaire against all manner of the ills that might befall us. And, writing in the midst of this global pandemic, and the urgent ethical necessity for responsible sanitary practice, I am suddenly aware of my immense privilege in that until a month ago I thought of sanitation and contagion as symbolic rather than epidemiological fields. At this moment in time, clean and containment can protect us, not only as individuals but also as a community. I considered clean, until very recently, an ideological conceit, always wielded to designate something as dirty, soiled or polluted. In the case of Mary, her cleanliness has been waged all too often against the contamination threatened by Jews, or fallen women, or whomever. What I see fragmentarily now, however, is that clean obtains so forcefully conceptually because contagion is a very real thing. This is not to say that cultural discourses of contamination are always attached to genuine existential threats; more often than not they affix to racialized or gendered anxieties about the other. It is to say, however, that because the genuine contagion of disease and pollution can operate so virulently and indiscriminately that the idea of hygienic purity can do so much cultural work. Covid-19 might be a virus, without nation or creed and offer no identity save that of a devastating biological fact, but it took very little time for it to be declared the 'Chinese virus' and for Chinese people across the globe to be subject to racist attacks. The reality of a virus does not cancel out virality as a potent metaphor; rather, living in the virus's midst helps us to apprehend just why the metaphor of contagion can be itself contagious.

Writing in a moment of terrifying virality, my mind casts back to commodification of clean in Western popular culture in recent history. Most notably, the Japanese 'organizing consultant' Marie Kondō and the Canadian psychologist and guru Jordan Peterson have both spruiked cleanliness as a form of self-help and self-mastery, to extraordinary success. Kondō's *The Life Changing Magic of Tidying* promises that the decluttering of objects offers a path to the decluttering of the self, 'when your room is clean and uncluttered, you have no choice but to examine your inner state' (Kondō 2014, 24). Tidying is life changing, according to Kondō, because it enables the cleaner to confront the ties that bind: we hold on to the mess as it attaches us to our past desires as well as to our misguided fantasies of the future. Tidying helps us confront the now, so that 'your real life begins after putting your house in order' (Kondō 2014, 235). Kondō's book employs a myriad of anecdotes as to how this transformation occurs, arguing that tackling the intimate space of the home enables one to streamline the intimate space of the psyche. Her clients lose weight, they jettison husbands, and they quit joyless jobs. They are free of detritus, and the unfettered self emerges as a consequence. Strikingly, they tend to be women. In Kondō's account, it is women who seem the most troubled by stuff, and it is to them that the responsibility for its evacuation falls. Mess signifies, then, the unruliness of female consumption, which manifests itself in the chaotic home, the overweight body, and the bad marriage. Kondō describes the plight of one of her clients, a young woman who lived in mess but aspired to a life of aromatherapy and yoga in a 'room as tidy as a hotel suite'. After adopting the life-changing magic of tidying up, Kondō reports that 'freed from the depths of disorder, she emerged to find the feminine lifestyle to which she aspired' (Kondō 2014, 43). Laurie Ouellette, in her reading of Kondō, points out that 'untidiness signified by a chaotic surplus of household goods is not a personal choice but a manifestation of late-capitalism, including women's unrelenting double shift' (Ouellette 2019, 548). In Kondō's tidy world, women are trapped in chaos and are themselves chaotic. At the same time, to become the fulfilment of the feminine – neat, glowing, lean – it is on them to other themselves as order.

Jordan Peterson's injunction to clean is more martial than that of Kondō and is explicitly directed at young men whom he perceives as demoralised and disempowered by shifting gender norms. In *12 Rules for Life: An Antidote to Chaos*, Peterson exhorts the young man to tidy his room to manifest order and achieve mastery over the self. Jordan chastises his readers, 'If you cannot bring peace to your household, how dare you try to rule a city' (Peterson 2018, 158). This injunction to tidy might seem a strange place to start upon a project of manliness, given the usual association of cleaning and home with domesticity and femininity. But Peterson is not talking about home; he is talking about the household, the *oikos*. In pacifying the household, Peterson argues, the young man takes his place as a political actor in his first political theatre. The household is the microcosm in which he learns to govern, to tame chaos. This process will result, Peterson argues, in a 'less-corrupted soul', a soul unencumbered by chaos (Peterson 2018, 159). And for Peterson, chaos belongs to the feminine and requires the antidote of masculine order. Feminist scholars, such as myself, might rail against gendered categories of thought, might attempt to sift through the sediments of history to understand how they came to be, and in so doing we might attempt to undo their power. For Peterson, these efforts are moot, in response to those critics who challenge his aggregation of chaos and femininity he says, 'it's been represented like that forever. And there are reasons for it. You can't change it. It's not possible' (Bowles 2018). Well that is that then.

Kondō's best-selling dream of emancipation from psychic clutter and Peterson's best-selling account of how to contain the disordered feminine, however different, register the valency of clean. The desire to wipe away grime runs deep, even when we cannot actually locate the dirt. Until very recently, when we returned holus bolus to industrial-grade cleaning products in valiant attempts at genuine sanitation, the clean beauty and clean eating movements were gaining traction and making all manner of cleansing claims. The promises of both were, and presumably still are, freedom from 'nasties' as the advertisements have it. Clean consumption marketing locates omnipresent and hidden poisons in common household foods and products and suggests that only mindful practices of purchasing and ingestion will protect us. Recently, Gwyneth Paltrow's GOOP website published a book on clean beauty. On the cover, obviously, stands Gwyneth, in a white robe standing on a beach. The blurb implores us to remember that it does not matter how many pigments we place on our skin, how we might paint our face, 'we also know that beauty starts from within.' To manage this within, the hidden inside of ourselves, it is imperative that we purify ourselves internally, for 'the ways we navigate stress, environmental factors, rest and repair all affect our glow' (GOOP 2019). What is the glow? It is the physical manifestation of the real beauty that starts internally. If the insides are broken, then presumably the glow is very dull, or perhaps even expired. The promise of clean is that of radiance and illumination;

these are spiritualising ideas. The glow is as silly as the halo, and probably as telling. And never mind if the glow is elusive, GOOP sells a range of skincare products called GOOPGLOW, which for a not-small price help you attain this luminescence.

GOOP, Kondō and Peterson might seem like cheap targets, however wealthy they have become through their endeavours. The promises of tidy and clean that permeate commercial culture seem so facile, and so easily mocked, that I feel silly even pointing them out, especially during this terrifying pandemic. But these promises of purity, tidiness and cleanliness are symptomatic of our incapacity to sit in mess, and to dwell in the hybridity and complexity of our being, and our world. Gwyneth et al. are peddling hope that we can ward off danger through processes of purification. True, they differ in their articulation of danger. For Kondō, danger lies in the disorder of accumulation, by holding on to things we hold on to our flaws. Poignantly, in her book, she writes that 'many times when confronting my past during the tidying process I have been so ashamed' (Kondō 2014, 212). Tidying becomes an act of expiation, a confessional that leads to forgiveness. Peterson's dangerous terrain is the mess of gender fluidity, the disruption of masculine privilege. Make no mistake, he tells us, a young man unable to find a sexual partner and establish his natural place as head of a household is a risk to us all. Feminised chaos needs an antidote, and it begins with the young man tidying his room. In the GOOP universe, we are naturally pure and glowing beings who have been stunted by the predations of industrialised food production and mass-market beauty products. Our rightful selves shine, but we have to detox to do so. Each of them has a point, hence the traction. My house, at least, is full of nonsense things that I did not and do not need; we have too many things. We are right to be worried about angry young men disappointed that the world has not gifted them the sexual and civil authority they claim to be owed. I am not worried for the same reasons as Peterson, in that I am not concerned for their dignity, but I have good reason to fear the entitled incel violence that we saw on display in the deeds of Elliott Rodger in 2014 and Alek Manassian in 2018. And while I am not particularly concerned about parabens in my foundation or silicones in my shampoo (two of the nasties targeted by spruikers of clean beauty), I am of course aware of the environmental and nutritional impact of industrialised agriculture that provides food security for the Western world, at the same time as it degrades the environment and depletes biodiversity. The prophets of clean are not wrong to account for risk, or to enumerate threats. Their ethical failure lies in their promise that we can cleanse ourselves of danger, and in so doing produce ourselves as perfected sovereigns and saints. This is self-help as border control.

Mary is without stain because God was able to declare her so, as sovereign he was able to make her the exception, to suspend the law. These current discourses of self-purification transform the self into the sovereign, who grants herself an exception on the basis of her own correct activity and consumption. Or, perhaps, she fantasises that capitalism will provide the exception when it recognises her goodness. Cleanliness and wellness promise immunity, and separation from the 'nasties'. I fall for this all the time, which is why I beg your indulgence with what might seem like a hackneyed critique of stainlessness. I have talked of the profound feeling-knowledge that I experienced after childbirth. But I am full, also, of countless other feeling-knowledges that infuse my days. These affects are messier and murkier than that which occurred after the searing experience of early maternity, and so more naturalised and harder to notice. I long for purity, not in a Virgin Mary way, but I long for a self that is continent and united in inner and outer experiences. I fantasize myself constantly as someone who will get there, one day, with 'there' being a place of completion. I find myself so confusing, so contradictory, and so messy that I spend a lot of time projecting a future self who is unsullied and pure. In her beautiful essay 'Purity, Impurity and Separation', Maria Lugones helps the reader enter into the space of this desire to be clean. She argues that for the lover of purity, '*the fundamental assumption is that there is unity underlying multiplicity* (Lugones 1994, 463, emphasis in original). Even when we are not sure what this unity constitutes, where it lives or how it functions, whenever we seek the pure we commit to the dream of totality. But the world, and we ourselves, are 'curdled', according to Lugones, relationality and hybridity are constitutive of our beings.

Intellectually, of course, I think that purity is nonsense. I know I am curdled. But it is a measure of the impurity of my curdledness that my desires still seek psychic absolutism. I am not even able to be purely impure; my mind desperately fixates on potential futures of liberation that would protect me from the untidiness of being a human. And so I dwell, feverishly, in fantasies of bodily transformation. I have had the same-looking body, more or less, since I was eleven. But, obdurately and unbidden, I fantasize a pure lean body as a possibility that if achieved would protect me from life's ravages. I look at people with those bodies, bodies that seem to me to be armoured and sealed, and feel that they are blessed somehow, that they have attained a form of purity unavailable to me. I am obsessed with bourgeois markers of taste, aspiring to live in the right type of house and wear the style of clothes that will make me safe somehow. From what? I have no idea what taste protects me from; I cannot even source the threat psychologically. But I consume out of the fear, and invariably the sought-after objects fail to provide the surety that I was after. And so I consume some more. I sit often in what Lauren Berlant has called cruel optimism, 'the condition of maintaining an attachment to an object *in advance of its loss*' (Berlant 2006, 21, emphasis in original). That is, I fret about and obsess upon an idea of myself that can only give me grief and be disappointing. And yet the libidinal pleasures of the fantasy that I can be pure in beauty and taste seem impossible to jettison, as do the fleeting consumptive satisfactions they engender when I buy more things in the aspiration. If affect gives you away, then I can tell you that my heart quickens in *Sephora*, or that I feel strangely psychologically light when I am on a diet. The lipstick, the diet, they offer short-term frissons that are enlivening, and they briefly displace complexity and mess. Cruel optimism, briefly, helps me to feel in control. But it does not lead to my flourishing, because the lipstick and the diet always let me down; I remain sad in myself, still furious at my impurity. The lipstick and the diet have not given me any resources for sitting with or engaging with my animal creaturely dirtiness. Instead, I am more distressed as I rage against the folly of my fantasy once again. I agree with Lugones that the love of purity results in a desire to control. Where I part ways with her is that I do not think that the love of purity emerges from a sense of unity but rather is a displacement of the gnawing existential impossibility of unity. I seek purity because it is too hard to be impure, and capitalism and scholarship are so good at helping me fend off the discomfort.

My examples of my own desire for purity, as they emerge in anxiety about myself, and things that I own might seem banal. Certainly, I bore myself with these longings, with my tedious orientation towards fortifying myself with appearances. Relating these desires feels very risky, in their seeming smallness, in their pettiness. But I do so because I am reminded of how *Ineffabilis Deus* described Mary's stainlessness as enabling her to be both 'ornament' and 'stronghold'. These are odd linguistic bedfellows. Mary as ornament requires that she be beautiful, that she be decorous. A stronghold, on the other hand, is a fortified place of defence. Normally, a stronghold is pragmatic and monu-mental, designed to protect rather than decorate. But this Marian formulation of the Immaculate Conception binds together seemliness and strength. Mary's purity makes her beautiful, and her beauty enables her to fortify and repel pollution. These are two of purity's most pernicious promises, that through perfection we are able to repel toxins, that we become impermeable and safe. My own story, I hope, is meaningful in its littleness. Purity's promise is intoxicating to me, in spite of its impossibility and its perversity. But I know, also, that the fantasy of purity is a corrosive one, one that separates people from each other, as well as their messy habitats. Owning up to my desire for purity is part of a practice of resistance to it, a resistance that will always be imperfect and contingent but which is far better than naturalising clean. Here I hear Sara Ahmed ringing in my ears. In *Living a Feminist Life*, she described the confronting difficulty of doing diversity work in institutional contexts, on the necessary impurity that comes with a genuine commitment to difference. She says 'we also have to accept our complicity, we forgo any illusions of purity; we give up the safety of exteriority . . . . Diversity work is messy, even dirty, work' (Ahmed 2017, 194). Purity not only alienates us from ourselves; it also wrestles us away from relational hard politics.

In an interview, Alexis Shotwell, author of *Against Purity*, had this to say on purity's dangerous purchase: 'it fundamentally comes back to the idea that the individual is a self-governing unit who can make decisions about what comes in and what goes out' (qtd. in Beck 2017). Mary is part of the story of how we got to this in the West. She is not the whole story; she is not the everything. My truth claim here is not to mark a boundary or to make a case for the acuity of my own noticing. Rather, the Immaculate Conception enables us to meditate upon the Virgin, as people have done for centuries before or us. Perhaps we might meditate upon her to help ourselves embrace the stain, not as something that ever needs to be cleaned, but as that which makes us uncomfortably, perpetually and stunningly dirty.

Conclusion

> Even for those of us who have never seen, or no longer see the world through Mary, reflection on her power to inspire and confuse and amaze and stifle, is an important and useful part of our reflection on what the maternal, and the historical, might mean to us today. (Rubin 2004, 16)

In this Element, I have tried to do exactly what Rubin suggests and reflect upon Mary's power, particularly when she is deployed to shame and to stifle. Mary, as she was produced by scholastic theology, was evacuated of the wretchedness that was understood to constitute humanity generally, and women in greater measure. Her perfection emptied her out. She was sexually pure, free of pain and utterly clean. She had no shame, no pain and no stain. And she had no agency in her perfection; it was granted to her by a sovereign God who did so because he could. She was the exception who proved his rule, because to make a woman immaculate could only be the work of omnipotence – the concept was so impossible otherwise. This Mary is fortified and perfect, and her purity is charged with repelling contamination and fortifying orthodoxy. Mary was made into this figure by thinkers, themselves engaged in a sanitising and shaming project. Scholastic theology aimed to clean up Christendom, and to make shameful those who refused their hygienic work. This was stifling work; it was a policing discourse that made clear where truth could be found and, by implication, where it could not. Women's bodies and women's experiences were not places where truth could be found, except as registers of sin. Mary's perfection made this clear.

Following Rubin, what does this mean for us today? Or following Ahmed, what is sticky about Mary? To what does she adhere? At the moment, in the cultural life of the West, she does often radical work. We have all seen Madonna in the video for her song *Like a Virgin* using Marian imagery to express carnality and desire. When Beyoncé announced her pregnancy with twins, and their subsequent births, she collaborated with visual artists to depict herself as the Virgin, styled as the black Madonna. The front page of the *New York Post* carried the pregnancy picture, and the headline read 'Beymaculate Conception'. And in an act of extraordinarily brave blasphemy, in 2012, Pussy Riot performed their punk prayer, before the altar of Moscow's Christ the Saviour Cathedral, in which they demanded of Mary 'virgin birth-giver of God, drive away Putin.' The Virgin can be a taboo buster; her putative sacredness offers a site for strategic, radical and ludic transgression.

So why am I being such a killjoy? Why not revel in Mary's generative capacities and explore how she is used for sacrilege and spoliation? Why not enumerate all that Mary disrupts, all that she troubles, how wicked she can be? Why have I stuck to the sacred Virgin when the profane version is so much more fun? I enjoy dirty messy Mary so much more than her beatific alter ego; why suffer in misery's company? To answer this question, I offer the words of Nora Fanshaw, a character in Noah Baumbach's 2019 film *Marriage Story*. Nora is a divorce lawyer, and she delivers a lecture to Nicole, her client, in which she explains how a mother should behave during custody negotiations. Nicole expresses to Nora her desire to acknowledge her own flaws as a mother, as well as her keenness to recognise the parenting skills of her soon-to-be ex-husband. Nora is having none of it; she tells Nicole that while we can accept an imperfect father, we cannot tolerate imperfections in mothers. Nora explains:

> We don't accept it structurally and we don't accept it spiritually because the basis of our Judeo-Christian Whatever is Mary Mother of Jesus and she's PERFECT. She's a virgin who gives birth, unwaveringly supports her child, and holds his dead body when he's gone. But the Dad isn't there. He didn't even do the fucking because God's in heaven. God is the father and God didn't show up so you have to be perfect. (Baumbach 2019)

I stick to the sacred Virgin in this Element, and she sticks to me, because of 'our Judeo-Christian whatever'. In this 'whatever', implausible and immaculate Mary persists to embody the vicious and viscous hold of impossible expectations of feminine perfection. The scholastics may have made her so, but we cannot blame them for her stamina and endurance into the present – they are long gone.

References

Adams, Marilyn McCord. 'The Immaculate Conception of the Blessed Virgin Mary: A Thought-Experiment in Medieval Philosophical Theology.' *Harvard Theological Review* 103 2 (2010): 133–59.

Ahmed, Sara. 'Affective Economies.' *Social Text* 79 (Summer 2004): 117–39.

Living a Feminist Life. Durham, NC: Duke University Press, 2017.

Queer Phenomenology: Orientations, Objects, Others. Durham NC: Duke University Press, 2006.

Asad, Talal. 'Notes on Body Pain and Truth in Medieval Christian Ritual.' *Economy and Society* 12 3 (1983): 287–327.

Augustine. *The Confessions* Maria Boulding, trans. New York: Random House, 1998.

Bartlett, Robert. *Trial by Fire and Water: The Medieval Judicial Ordeal*. Oxford: Clarendon, 1986.

Battersby, Christine. *The Phenomenal Woman: Feminist Metaphysics and the Patterns of Identity*. Cambridge: Polity Press, 1998.

Beattie, Tina. *God's Mother, Eve's Advocate*. New York: Continuum Books, 2002.

Beck, Julie. 'The Folly of Purity Politics.' *The Atlantic* 20 January 2017. Accessed 15 November 2019. www.theatlantic.com/health/archive/2017/01/purity-politics/513704/

Berlant, Lauren. 'Cruel Optimism.' *Differences* 17 3 (2006): 20–36.

Boss, Sarah Jane, ed. *Mary: The Complete Resource*. New York: Continuum Books 2007.

Boureau, Alain. 'Privilege in Medieval Societies from the Twelfth to the Fourteenth Centuries, or: How the Exception Proves the Rule.' In Peter Linehan and Janet L. Nelson, eds. *The Medieval World*. London: Routledge, 2001. 621–34.

Bourke, Joanna. *The Story of Pain: From Prayer to Painkillers*. Oxford: Oxford University Press, 2014.

Bowles, Nellie. 'Jordan Peterson: Custodian of the Patriarchy' *New York Times*. 18 May 2018. Accessed 31 March 2020. www.nytimes.com/2018/05/18/style/jordan-peterson-12-rules-for-life.html

Burrus, Virginia. *Saving Shame: Martyrs, Saints and Other Abject Subjects*. Philadelphia: University of Pennsylvania Press, 2008.

Cavarero, Adriana. '"A Child Has Been Born Unto Us": Arendt on Birth.' *philoSOPHIA* 4 1 (2014): 12–30.

Cohen, Esther. *The Modulated Scream: Pain in Late Medieval Culture.* Chicago: Chicago University Press, 2009.

Clueless. Directed by Amy Heckerling (Los Angeles: Paramount, 1995).

Cohen, Andrew. 'The Torture Memos, 10 Years Later' *The Atlantic.* 6 February 2012. Accessed 15 November 2019. www.theatlantic.com/national/archive/2012/02/the-torture-memos-10-years-later/252439/

Colish, Marcia L. *Peter Lombard.* Leiden: E.J. Brill, 1994.

Cosmopolitan. September 1988. US edn.

Crocker, Holly A. 'Medieval Affects Now.' *Exemplaria* 29 1 (2017): 82–98.

Cross, Richard. *Duns Scotus.* New York: Oxford University Press, 1999.

Edgar, Swift, and Angela M. Kinney, eds. *The Vulgate Bible: Douay-Rheims Translation.* Cambridge, MA: Harvard University Press, 2010.

Every, Louis. 'St. Thomas' Explanation of the Hail Mary.' *Dominicana* 35 (1954): 31–8.

Ferrell, Robyn. *Copula Sexual Technologies, Reproductive Powers.* Albany: State University of New York Press. 2006.

Foucault, Michel. *The History of Sexuality*, Vol. I. Robert Hurley, trans. New York: Pantheon Books, 1978.

Freud, Sigmund. *The Psychology of Love.* Shaun Whiteside, trans. London: Penguin Books, 2007.

Gambero, Luigi. *Mary in the Middle Ages: The Blessed Virgin Mary in the Thought of Medieval Latin Theologians.* San Francisco: Ignatius Press, 2005.

Gatens, Moira. *Imaginary Bodies Ethics, Power and Corporeality.* London: Routledge, 1996.

Glancy, Jennifer A. *Corporal Knowledge: Early Christian Bodies.* Oxford: Oxford University Press, 2010.

Goop. 'What is Clean Beauty & Why is it so Important?' Goop.Com. Accessed 15 November 2019. https://goop.com/beauty/personal-care/clean-beauty-and-why-its-important/

Hadley, Tessa. 'Mothers by Jacqueline Rose – Review: An Indignant Defence.' *Guardian.* 20 April 2018. Accessed 15 November 2019. www.theguardian.com/books/2018/apr/20/mothers-jacqueline-rose-review

Highmore, Ben. 'Bitter Aftertaste.' In Melissa Gregg and Gregory J. Seigworth, eds. *The Affect Theory Reader.* Durham, NC: Duke University Press, 2010: 118–37.

Kelly, Mary. *Post-Partum Document.* London: Routledge & Kegan Paul, 1983.

Klein, Linda Kay. *Pure: Inside the Evangelical Movement That Shamed a Generation of Young Women and How I Broke Free.* New York: Atria Books, 2018.

Kondō, Marie. *The Life-Changing Magic of Tidying: The Japanese Art of Decluttering and Organizing*. Cathy Hirano, trans. London: Random House, 2014.

Kristeva, Julia. 'Stabat Mater.' Ben Goldhammer, trans. *Poetics Today* 6 1/2 (1985): 133–52.

Leo XIII. *Rerum Novarum* 1891. Accessed 15 November 2019. www.vatican.va/content/leo-xiii/en/encyclicals/documents/hf_l-xiii_enc_15051891_rerum-novarum.html

Lepore, Jill. 'The Deadline (Friendship and Loss).' *The New Yorker* 1 July 2019. Accessed 15 November 2019. www.newyorker.com/magazine/2019/07/08/the-lingering-of-loss

Leys, Ruth. 'The Turn to Affect: A Critique.' *Critical Inquiry* 37 3 (2011): 434–72.

Lloyd, Genevieve. *The Man of Reason: 'Male' and 'Female' in Western Philosophy*. London: Methuen, 1984.

Lombard, Peter. *The Sentences Book 2: On Creation*. Giulio Silano, trans. Toronto: Pontifical Institute of Mediaeval Studies, 2009.

Lugones, Maria. 'Purity, Impurity, and Separation.' *Signs* 19 2 (1994): 458–79.

Malti-Douglas, Fedwa. *Encyclopedia of Sex and Gender*. Detroit: Macmillan Reference, 2007.

Monagle, Clare, 'Christ's Masculinity: Homo and Vir in Peter Lombard's Sentences.' In Susan Broomhall, ed. *Ordering Emotions in Europe, 1100–1800*. Leiden: E.J. Brill, 2015. 32–47.

Orthodoxy and Controversy in Twelfth-Century Religious Discourse: Peter Lombard's 'Sentences' and the Development of Theology. Turnhout, Belgium: Brepols, 2013.

The Scholastic Project. Kalamazoo: ARC Humanities Press, 2017.

New Catholic Encyclopedia Supplement 2012–13: Ethics and Philosophy. Farmington Hills, MI: Gale, 2013.

Noel, Gabrielle. 'Miley Cyrus is right – there is no such thing as virginity.' *Independent* Tuesday 16 July 2019. Accessed 15 November 2019. www.independent.co.uk/voices/miley-cyrus-virginity-social-construct-mother-s-daughter-a9006816.html

Orloff, Brian. 'Miley Cyrus wants to make "Cleaner" Sex and the City.' *People* 15 July 2008. Accessed 15 November 2019. https://people.com/celebrity/miley-cyrus-wants-to-make-cleaner-sex-and-the-city/

Ouellette, Laurie. 'Spark Joy? Compulsory Happiness and the Feminist Politics of Decluttering.' *Culture Unbound* 11 3–4 (2019): 534–50.

Peterson, Jordan B., Doidge, Norman, and Van Sciver, Ethan. *12 Rules for Life: An Antidote for Chaos*. London: Allen Lane, 2018.

Remensnyder, Amy G. 'Christian Captives, Muslim Maidens, and Mary.' *Speculum* 82 3 (2007): 642–77.

Rich, Adrienne. *Of Woman Born: Motherhood as Experience and Institution.* New York: Norton, 1976.

Robinson, Emily. 'Touching the Void: Affective History and the Impossible.' *Rethinking History* 14 4 (2010): 503–20.

Rose, Jacqueline. *Mothers: An Essay on Love and Cruelty.* New York: Farrar, Straus and Giroux, 2018.

Rosemann, Philipp W. *Peter Lombard.* Oxford: Oxford University Press, 2004.

Rubin, Miri. 'Mary.' *History Workshop Journal* 58 1 (2004): 1–16.

Scarry, Elaine. *The Body in Pain: The Making and Unmaking of the World.* New York: Oxford University Press, 1985.

Schaefer, Donovan O. *Religious Affects: Animality, Evolution, and Power.* Durham, NC: Duke University Press, 2015.

Schmitt, Carl. *Political Theology: Four Chapters on the Concept of the Political.* Chicago: University of Chicago Press, 2005.

Sedgwick, Eve Kosofsky. *Touching Feeling: Affect, Pedagogy, Performativity.* Durham, NC: Duke University Press, 2003.

Sedgwick, Eve Kosofsky, Frank, Adam. 'Shame in the Cybernetic Fold: Reading Silvan Tomkins.' *Critical Inquiry* 21 2 (1995): 496–522.

Smalley, Beryl. *Studies in Medieval Thought and Learning from Abelard to Wyclif.* London: Hambledon Press, 1981.

Solberg, Emma Maggie. *Virgin Whore.* Ithaca: Cornell University Press, 2018.

Spiegel, Gabrielle, M. 'History, Historicism, and the Social Logic of the Text in the Middle Ages.' *Speculum* 65 1 (1990): 59–86.

Stanglin, Keith D. *The Reformation to the Modern Church.* Minneapolis: Fortress Press, 2014.

Stewart, Kathleen. 'Worlding Refrains.' In Melissa Gregg and Gregory J. Seigworth, eds. *The Affect Theory Reader.* Durham, NC: Duke University Press, 2010: 339–53.

Talladega Nights: The Ballad of Ricky Bobby. Directed by Adam McKay (Los Angeles: Sony, 2006).

Tanner, Norman P. ed. and trans. *The Decrees of the Ecumenical Councils* Vol. I. London: Sheed & Ward, 1990.

Tappest, T. G. *The Book of Concord.* Philadelphia: Fortress Press, 1959.

Thompson, Janet. *Praying for Your Prodigal Daughter: Hope, Help and Encouragement for Hurting Parents.* New York: Howard Books, 2007.

Tomkins, Silvan. *Affect Imagery Consciousnes.* Vol. II: *The Negative Affects.* New York: Springer, 1963.

Vogel, Carol. 'The Met Makes its Biggest Purchase Ever.' *The New York Times*. 10 November 2004. Accessed 15 November 2019. www.nytimes.com/2004/11/10/arts/design/the-met-makes-its-biggest-purchase-ever.html

Warner, Marina. *Alone of All Her Sex: The Myth and the Cult of the Virgin Mary*. London: Weidenfeld and Nicolson, 1976.

Warner, Michael. *The Trouble with Normal: Sex, Politics and the Ethics of Queer Life*. New York: The Free Press, 1999.

Whitburn, L. Y., Jones, Lester E., Davey, Mary-Ann, McDonald, Susan. 'The Nature of Labour Pain: An Updated Review of the Literature.' *Women and Birth* 32 1 (2019): 28–38.

Williams, Thomas. 'John Duns Scotus.' *The Stanford Encyclopedia of Philosophy*. Edward N. Zalta, ed. Accessed 15 November 2019. https://plato.stanford.edu/entries/duns-scotus/

Wolter, Allan B. *Four Questions on Mary*. Bonaventure, NY: Franciscan Institute Publications, 2000.

Acknowledgements

I owe thanks to the two anonymous reviewers of this manuscript, who offered advice and criticism that I have taken to heart and mind in reviewing this text. Jan Plamper's editorial work has been so thoughtful and engaged. He is very generous. He read the work closely, identified problems and, most crucially, he offered ideas as to how to solve them.

I need to thank my colleagues at Macquarie who read and commented upon sections of the text, and provided encouragement and kindness when I showed them such personal work.

Barbara Caine invited me, in 2014, to join a terrifyingly accomplished group of women in a reading and writing group. They are Katherine Biber, Dany Celermajer, Moira Gatens, Helen Groth, Julia Kindt, Tess Lea and Glenda Sluga. These women helped me work through this work, and I'm grateful to Barbara in particular for her coordination of this amazing group of women into a reading community.

And, I need to recognise the support of the Sydney Scrags, who engaged with this work with empathy and tough love. Avril Alba, Anna Clark, Frances Flanagan, Kate Fullagar, Rebecca Sheehan, Zora Simic, Jesse Stein, Amanda Third and Jess Whyte are the Scrags, and this little Element would not exist without them.

In 2012, I was fortunate to receive a Discovery Early Career Research Award from the Australian Research Council. Although 2012 seems very long ago now, it was the time afforded by that grant that has enabled me to develop the ideas, and negotiate the feelings, that constitute *Scholastic Affect*.

Finally, my gratitude to the once-little, now 170 cm tall, Honora Carmel Monagle.

Cambridge Elements ≡

Histories of Emotions and the Senses

Jan Plamper

Goldsmiths, University of London

Jan Plamper is Professor of History at Goldsmiths, University of London, where
he teaches an MA seminar on the history of emotions. His publications include
The History of Emotions: An Introduction (2015), a multidisciplinary volume on fear with
contributors from neuroscience to horror film to the 1929 stock market crash,
and articles on the sensory history of the Russian Revolution and the history
of soldiers' fears in World War I. He has also authored *The Stalin Cult: A Study
in the Alchemy of Power* (2012) and, in German, *The New We. Why Migration is
No Problem: A Different History of the Germans* (2019).

About the Series

Born of the emotional and sensory 'turns,' Elements in Histories of Emotions
and the Senses move one of the fastest-growing interdisciplinary fields forward.
The series is aimed at scholars across the humanities, social sciences, and life
sciences, embracing insights from a diverse range of disciplines, from neuroscience to art
history and economics. Chronologically and regionally broad, encompassing global,
transnational, and deep history, it concerns such topics as affect theory, intersensoriality,
embodiment, human-animal relations, and distributed cognition.

Cambridge Elements ≡

Histories of Emotions and the Senses

Elements in the Series

The Evolution of Affect Theory: The Humanities, the Sciences,
and the Study of Power
Donovan O. Schaefer

Satire and the Public Emotions
Robert Phiddian

Newborn Imitation: The Stakes of a Controversy
Ruth Leys

Scholastic Affect: Gender, Maternity and the History of Emotions
Clare Monagle

A full series listing is available at: www.cambridge.org/EHES